A Bilingual Library
Contemporary Chinese Master Writers

当 代 中 国 名 家
双 语 阅 读 文 库

丛 书 主 编 | 许诗焱 杨昊成
丛书副主编 | 李钟涛

JIA

PING

WA

贾平凹

作凹题

| 卷 |

南京师范大学出版社
NANJING NORMAL UNIVERSITY PRESS

图书在版编目（CIP）数据

当代中国名家双语阅读文库. 贾平凹卷：汉英对照 /
贾平凹著；许诗焱，杨昊成主编. — 南京：南京师范
大学出版社，2020.10
ISBN 978-7-5651-4722-7

I.①当… Ⅱ.①贾… ②许… ③杨… Ⅲ.①中国文
学－当代文学－作品综合集－汉、英　Ⅳ.①I217.1

中国版本图书馆 CIP 数据核字（2020）第 176700 号

丛 书 名	当代中国名家双语阅读文库
丛书主编	许诗焱　杨昊成
书　　名	当代中国名家双语阅读文库·贾平凹卷
著　　者	贾平凹
译　　者	Denis Mair, Jun Liu(刘浚), Nick Stember, Annelise Finegan Wasmoen, Ella Schwalb
封面题字	徐　燕
策划编辑	郑海燕　王雅琼
责任编辑	王雅琼
出版发行	南京师范大学出版社
地　　址	江苏省南京市玄武区后宰门西村 9 号(邮编:210016)
电　　话	(025)83598919(总编办)　83598412(营销部) 83373872(邮购部)
网　　址	http://press.njnu.edu.cn
电子信箱	nspzbb@njnu.edu.cn
照　　排	南京开卷文化传媒有限公司
印　　刷	江苏凤凰通达印刷有限公司
开　　本	880 毫米×1230 毫米　1/32
印　　张	8.875
字　　数	187 千
版　　次	2020 年 10 月第 1 版　2020 年 10 月第 1 次印刷
书　　号	ISBN 978-7-5651-4722-7
定　　价	38.00 元
出 版 人	张志刚

贾平凹

1952 年出生于陕西丹凤县棣花镇，1973 年开始发表作品，1975 年毕业于西北大学中文系。现为全国人大代表、中国作家协会副主席、陕西省作家协会主席、《延河》《美文》杂志主编。代表作有《废都》《秦腔》等长篇小说，《黑氏》《美穴地》等中短篇小说及《丑石》《商州三录》等散文。作品曾多次获得茅盾文学奖、鲁迅文学奖等国家级文学奖，被翻译为英、法、德、俄、日、韩、越等 30 多个语种，被改编为电影、电视、话剧、戏剧等 20 余种。

Jia Pingwa

He was born in 1952 in Dihua Village, Danfeng County, Shaanxi Province. He began publishing in 1973, and graduated from the Chinese Language and Literature Department at Northwest University in 1975. Jia is a current member of the National People's Congress, vice-chairman of China Writers' Association, chairman of Writers' Association of Shaanxi Province, and editor-in-chief of *Yanhe* and *Meiwen* magazines. Published representative works include novels such as *Ruined City* and *Qin Opera*, short stories "A Woman Named Black," "Felicitous Site," and essays "The Ugly Rock," "Three Chapters about Shangzhou," and more. His works have won many national literature prizes such as Mao Dun Literature Prize and Lu Xun Literature Prize. His works have been translated and published in more than 30 languages including English, French, German, Russian, Japanese, Korean, and Vietnamese, and have been adapted for film, television, theater, and opera over 20 times.

—

总　序

近年来，中国文学外译以前所未有的蓬勃势头展开。在江苏省委宣传部的直接领导下，南京师范大学外国语学院与江苏省作家协会、凤凰出版传媒集团合作，于 2014 年 4 月在伦敦书展上推出全英文期刊《中华人文》，之后又与南京师范大学出版社合作，于 2018 年推出《当代中国名家双语阅读文库》（第一辑）。这无疑

Preface

In recent years, translation of Chinese literature has gained unprecedented momentum. With the support of the Publicity Department of Jiangsu Provincial Party Committee, in cooperation with Writers' Association of Jiangsu Province and Phoenix Publishing & Media Group, the School of Foreign Languages and Cultures at Nanjing Normal University launched *Chinese Arts & Letters*, a journal introducing Chinese literature in translation to English-language readers in April, 2014. In 2018, the School of Foreign Languages and Cultures at Nanjing Normal University collaborated with Nanjing Normal University Press to launch the first volume of

是中国文学"走出去"的一次主动尝试。

杨昊成教授之前一直担任《中华人文》和《当代中国名家双语阅读文库》（以下简称《文库》）的主编，然而，2018 年 10 月他不幸因病去世。杨昊成教授生前一直饱受病痛之扰，但他始终追求卓越，不仅逐字逐句审读这两份出版物中的每一篇文章，对于封面设计、文字配图等细节也都亲力亲为。《文库》的总序原来由杨昊成教授撰写，作为继任者，我理应对总序稍加修改，并表达对杨昊成教授的感谢和怀念。

对于这个文库，至少有两点可以一说。首先，它是在中国文化"走出去"这个时代背景下诞生的，这对于《文库》的出版意义重大。一个国家在世界经济中获得坚强地位后——正如中国强有力地向外部世界所展示的那样，就希望在诸如文化等其他各个方面全面出击，这是很正常的事。从历史上看，法语联盟、英国文化协会、歌德学院等都是这样，它们都是各自国家从事文化交流的重镇。虽说它们多半是民族自信和自豪的产物，但它们的存在似乎完全没有错。关键问题还是在于一个国家的文化如何走出

A Bilingual Library of Contemporary Chinese Master Writers. This work is a vibrant initiative of Chinese literature Going Global.

Professor Yang Haocheng was the editor-in-chief of *Chinese Arts & Letters* and *A Bilingual Library of Contemporary Chinese Master Writers* until he passed away in October, 2018. He had suffered from serious illnesses all his life, yet always continued to pursue excellence. Not only did he read every word of all the pieces printed in both publications, but he also devoted himself to the details of cover design and selection of illustrations. This Preface was originally written by Professor Yang. As his successor, I am revising it, and I would like to express my gratitude to him. I dearly cherish his memory.

There are two things that must be said. First, the present *Library* was born amidst the favorable climate of Chinese culture Going Global which was a significant factor in its publication. It is natural that when a country has earned a stronghold in the world economy, as China has now done so robustly, it will desire to go all out in other respects, including culture. Historically, it has been true of such institutions as the Alliance Française, the British Council, and the Goethe-Institut, all important channels for their respective countries' cultural flow and interaction. It is probably a matter of national self-confidence and pride, but there is nothing wrong with that. The question that remains is how a country's culture should go global. Two forces are at work: various

去。有两股力量在做着这方面的工作：一是各级官员，二是诸如学者、作家、翻译家、编辑等专业人士。这两股力量有着同一个目标，但在将自己的文化成就介绍到外部世界去的时候，他们所采取的策略和手段却不尽相同。前者中不乏不通外语及外国文化者，想把自己认为的宝贝强行兜售给潜在的买家，殊不知文化交流很大程度上犹如贸易，是建立在平等交换及买家自愿选择的基础之上的，任何一厢情愿的强卖是注定要失败的。后者比前者要更懂行，却在政治方向和经济资助上有赖于前者，因此常常陷入这样一种困境：他们想按自己认为的正确的道路前进，却不时遭遇不受欢迎的指示或干扰。《中国文学》这份挣扎了整整五十年的官方杂志就是一个很好的教训。虽然《中国文学》在它的后半段有杨宪益这样多产又具有人格魅力的翻译家担任主编，但杨宪益一人显然无力抵御他那个时代的政治影响。《中国文学》有着明显的时代印记，这也解释了为什么这么多年它在海外一直不怎么为人所接受。

非常幸运的是，《文库》得以坚持自己既定的标准，《文

bureaucrats, and professionals such as researchers, writers, translators, editors, and publishers. The two forces have the same aim, but each espouses different strategies and approaches for introducing their cultural achievements to the outside world. Some ignorant of the foreign languages and their cultures, bureaucrats want very much to sell what they deem to be precious material to a potential buyer, not knowing that cultural exchange is, to a great extent, like trade and is built on the basis of equal give-and-take and willingness on the side of the buyer, while any one-sided forced selling is doomed to fail. Though much more informed, the professionals are reliant on the bureaucrats for political direction and financial support, and are thus left in a dilemma. They want to proceed with what they regard as the right path, but are frequently met with undesirable obstacles, including unwelcomed directions or interferences from the bureaucrats. The case of *Chinese Literature*, an officially sponsored magazine that has struggled for a full fifty years, is instructive. Though *Chinese Literature* has had as its chief editor the prolific, charismatic translator Yang Xianyi for the second half of its fifty-year life, Yang alone certainly would not have had sufficient strength to stay clear of the political influences of his day. *Chinese Literature* bears the clear hallmark of its time, which explains its low readership overseas over the years.

Fortunately, the present *Library* is able to adhere to its set standard, and what is collected here are either representative works

库》内收集的都是当今中国最负盛名的作家的代表作或得到人们高度认可的作品。数十年的意识形态斗争过去了，我们终于可以回归到文学创作的本体研究。所有收录在本文库的翻译作品，虽然它们对待文学的手法和角度有着天壤之别，却都道出了人性和人生的共性，那就是人类的喜、怒、哀、乐。这些短篇，以其洗练的笔法、精巧的结构、典型的人物事件，成为当代中国文学宝库中极为重要的组成部分。为了更好更立体地呈现作家及其作品，除了少数例外，我们还为每个作家收录了一篇评论和一篇访谈。

其次，从事翻译的人都清楚，当目标语为母语时，译者们做得就要好一些。译者的母语是英语，从事汉译英就会得心应手得多，这是不争的事实。杨昊成老师曾就《水浒传》的翻译给沙博理先生（Sidney Shapiro）打电话，电话中沙博理先生非常坦诚地表示："对我来说，翻译像《水浒传》这样的作品比将英文材料译成中文要容易得多。虽然早在1963年我就入了中国籍，但中文毕竟不是我的母语。"

本文库以拥有一支高超的职业翻译家队伍为豪，他们的母语

or highly recognized pieces of some of the most famous writers from contemporary China. After the lapse of dozens of years of ideological struggles, we are able to return at last to the ontological study of literary creation, and all the works translated here speak of the commonality of human nature and human life—humankind's happiness, anger, sorrow, and joy—despite their vastly different approaches and perspectives toward literature. With their succinct style, exquisite structure, and typical characters and events, these stories constitute an extremely important, integral part of the treasure house of contemporary Chinese literature. For a better, more three-dimensional presentation of the authors and their works, we have also included a critique and an interview for each author, with only a few exceptions.

In addition, it is common knowledge among translators that they do better when translating into their mother tongue. It's an undeniable fact that translators whose mother tongue is English will be much more at home when it comes to Chinese-English translation. Professor Yang Haocheng used to call Sidney Shapiro about his translation of *Outlaws of the Marsh*. Mr. Shapiro once said to him on the phone, "Translating things like *Outlaws of the Marsh* is much easier for me than translating English materials into Chinese. After all, Chinese is not my mother tongue, though I became a Chinese citizen all the way back in 1963. "

The present *Library* boasts a terrific pool of professional

是英语，又全都是双语或多种语言的使用者。他们同时也都是《中华人文》的译者。这就完全不一样了。事实上，无论是《中国文学》还是几乎所有其他由中国人办的期刊杂志，都有着相同的问题：它们的译者大都是非母语使用者，其英语是作为第二语言习得的，无法跟母语是英语的职业翻译家相比。更为难得的是，这些译者对中文的掌握都是一流的，其中不少人是世界公认的汉学家或老牌的中国通。Denis Mair（梅丹理）、Nicky Harman（韩斌）、Natascha Bruce、Luisetta Mudie、Shelly Bryant（白雪莉）、Josh Stenberg（石峻山）、Helen Wang、Jeremy Tiang、Eric Abrahamsen、Michael Day、Simon Patton、Florence Woo 等，是我们最为尽职而宝贵的翻译家中的一部分。出自他们之手的译作，乍看之下可能并无特殊之处，实际却很是地道，常令我们击节叹赏。

因此，《文库》的目标读者首先是对翻译感兴趣的读者，尤其是学习翻译的本科生和研究生。杨昊成老师在审阅译稿时，时常忍不住把译者的精彩译文抄录下来，并加以点评："她有着凹凸有致的身材"译为 "She has a figure of voluptuous curves"。还

translators whose mother tongue is English, and all of them are bilingual or multilingual. They are the same translators who are working for *Chinese Arts & Letters*. This makes all the difference. In fact, both *Chinese Literature* and almost all other journals and magazines run by Chinese publishers have the same problem. Many of their translators are non-native speakers or writers of the target language, and their English was learned as a second language. They cannot be compared with professional translators whose mother tongue is English and, better still, whose command of the Chinese language is superb. Many of them are internationally recognized sinologists or old China hands to boot. Denis Mair, Nicky Harman, Natascha Bruce, Luisetta Mudie, Shelly Bryant, Josh Stenberg, Helen Wang, Jeremy Tiang, Eric Abrahamsen, Michael Day, Simon Patton, and Florence Woo are among our most conscientious and treasured translators. What comes out of their hands may seem at first glance to be nothing special, yet their work is so idiomatic that we cannot help but admire.

The target audience of the present *Library,* then, should first of all be readers interested in translation, especially undergraduates and graduate students studying translation. When Professor Yang Haocheng was reading the manuscripts prepared by these translators, he often could not keep himself from copying their wonderful translations with careful analysis, such as the rendering of, "她有着凹凸有致的身材"（meaning "She has a figure of

有一个高度口语化的专门词语可以用来描述这样的女孩，即
zaftig，所以我们经常可以听到人们说：她是那种身材火辣、招
蜂引蝶的女孩儿（She is a sort of zaftig, coquettish girl）。"包二
奶"如今已是很常见的一个说法了，我们的译者将它译成"to
keep a bit on the side"，"当小三"也就顺理成章地译作"to be
sb's bit on the side"；bit 意为"水性杨花的女子"，on the side 意
思是"悄悄地""私下里"，不过还带点幽默。如今许多年轻人喜
欢用的"吃货"一词，在英文里也有相对应的说法，即"greedy
guts"［注意是 guts 而非 gut，如 He is a greedy guts（他是个吃
货)]，虽然在已故陆谷孙教授主编的《中华汉英大词典》中有诸
如 foodie、glutton、gourmand、gastronaut、food aficionado 等其他
译法。"恶搞"（to kuso）事实上来自日语，但已进入英语词汇，
令 to parody、to lampoon、to snark 等稍显过时。phubber 是
phubbing 一词的逆构，据说是由澳大利亚的几个语言学家、词典
编纂家和作家从 phone 和 snub 两个词合并创立的一个新词。这个
新词用来描述那种不顾周围人事、一心看手机的人，和目前流行
的中国词语"低头族"完全一致。这个词只有几年的历史，尽管

voluptuous curves"). There is a special word, albeit highly colloquial, to describe that kind of girl, "zaftig." So we constantly hear people say, "She is a sort of zaftig, coquettish girl." Similarly, "包二奶" is a very common term today, and our translator renders it "to keep a bit on the side." Accordingly, "当小三" is "to be sb's bit on the side," "bit" meaning a loose woman, and "on the side," in secret or on the sly, but with a bit of humor. Likewise, "吃货," a term enjoyed by many young people today, has also its English equivalent, "greedy guts." (Mind you, it's *guts* and not *gut*. For instance: *He is a greedy guts.*) This is aside from other possible renderings, such as foodie, glutton, gourmand, gastronaut, or food aficionado, as listed by the *Chinese-English Dictionary* chief-editored by the late Professor Lu Gusun. And "恶搞" actually has a Japanese term "to kuso," which has already entered the English language, making "to parody," "to lampoon," and "to snark" seem somewhat outdated. "Phubber," the reverse formation of "phubbing," which is said to be a new coinage by some Australian linguists, lexicographers, and authors from "phone" and "snub," a neologism to describe the habit of snubbing people around you in favor of a mobile phone, is an exact equivalent of the the popular Chinese term "低头族." It only has a history of several years, and though already included in the *Australian National Dictionary*, most other dictionaries or thesauruses have not yet included it. And such simple oral sayings as "过了这村儿没这店儿" and "金窝银窝,不如自家狗

已被收入《澳大利亚国家词典》，其他绝大多数词典或工具书却尚未收入。简单而口语化的说法如"过了这村儿没这店儿"和"金窝银窝，不如自家狗窝"，被高超地译成了简洁有力的"It's now or never"，和至今为止最贴近原文的"Gold dish, silver dish, they cannot compare to your own dog's dish"，它们分别是从平淡无奇的"last chance"和同样令人难忘却丢失了原意象的"East or west, home is best"中生出的天才的产物。仅此一点就足以使本文库成为对翻译感兴趣的读者的一个很好的阅读材料。事实上，这些材料对我们编辑自己而言，也是一个了解两种语言以及全面提升自己的极好机会。目前已有不少高校使用本套《文库》作为笔译课程的教材，并将其列为翻译硕士考试的参考书目。

《文库》的目标读者还包括比较文学和中西文化比较研究的学者。在系统的规划、组织和支持下，中国文学作品外译输出的数量和质量都有了很大的提高，但中国文学的海外影响力仍然有限，尚未成为世界文学中的"活跃存在"。我们认为，解决这个问题的关键在于，不仅仅要关注中国文学的海外翻译，同时更要窝" are masterfully translated into the pithy phrase, "It's now or never," and the most faithful to date, "Gold dish, silver dish, they cannot compare to your own dog's dish," respectively, both genius outgrowths from the prosaic "last chance," and the equally memorable—though losing the image—clause, "East or west, home is best." This alone is a good reason why the *Library* is a good read for all who are interested in translation. In fact, editing these works has turned out to be a great opportunity for us editors to learn about the two languages, and it has generally uplifted us. Many universities have chosen the *Library* as the textbook for their translation courses and have included it in the list of reference books for the entrance examination for their Masters in Translation and Interpretation programs.

The target audience of the present *Library* also includes scholars of comparative literature and comparative study of the cultures of East and West. With systematic planning, organization, and support, the quantity and quality of translations of Chinese literature have greatly improved. However, their influence overseas is still limited, and Chinese literature in translation is still not an "active presence" in World Literature. We believe that the key to addressing this problem is to emphasize not only international translation of Chinese literature, but also international literary criticism. At the Symposium on Chinese Literature Going Global

注重中国文学的海外评论。在"从莫言获奖看中国文学如何走出去"学术会议上，宋炳辉教授指出："中国文学要真正走出去，其实在很大程度上还要依靠文学研究者对文学作品本身的阐释，对文学作品内涵的有效和多元阐释是实现本土文学国际化的一个重要因素。"在当代中国文学外译中，这一维度目前未受到应有的重视，而我们正努力在这方面有所突破。杨昊成教授去世之后，南京师范大学外国语学院邀请盛宁教授担任《中华人文》主编，对于《文库》的译介内容选择，尤其是访谈和评论的选择，盛宁教授都全程给予指导。盛宁教授曾担任我国外国文学研究顶级期刊《外国文学评论》主编，众多中国学者通过这一高端平台对外国文学进行多角度的解读与评论，极大地促进了外国文学在中国的"活跃存在"。我们希望通过《文库》，鼓励学者评论翻译成英语的、作为世界文学组成部分的中国文学。换句话说，盛宁教授以前工作的重心是引导学者用汉语评论外国文学，而现在则是引导更多的学者用外语评论中国文学，当然包括海外汉学家的评论。我们要让中国文学不但有效地"走出去"，而且能够真正

since Mo Yan won the Nobel Prize, Professor Song Binghui pointed out that "for Chinese literature to really go global, it must, to a large extent, depend on literary scholars' interpretation of the literary works, and having effective multiple interpretations of the literary works is an important factor in realizing the internationalization of local literature." When contemporary Chinese literature has been introduced to the world, this dimension has not received due attention, so we are trying to achieve a breakthrough in this area. After Professor Yang Haocheng passed away, we invited Professor Sheng Ning to be the editor-in-chief of *Chinese Arts & Letters*. Selection of the content for the *Library*, especially the interviews and criticisms, followed Professor Sheng Ning's suggestions. Professor Sheng Ning was formerly the editor-in-chief of *Foreign Literature Review*, the top-level journal in the field of foreign literature studies. On this platform, many Chinese scholars interpret and criticize foreign literature from various perspectives, facilitating the "active presence" of foreign literature in China. We hope that the *Library* will encourage scholars to criticize Chinese literature translated into English and as a part of World Literature. In other words, Professor Sheng Ning formerly focused on guiding scholars to criticize foreign literature in Chinese, but now he is focusing on guiding more scholars to criticize Chinese literature in foreign languages, including literary criticism from foreign sinologists. We hope to ensure that Chinese literature is not only

地"走进去"。

《文库》还希望能够引起译学界对文学翻译过程研究的关注。如前文所述,《文库》的译者均为母语为英语的海外汉学家;与此同时,依托南京师范大学外国语学院,选择专门从事文学、翻译研究的教师作为编辑,通过译者—编辑合作模式完成译稿。合作基本程序为译者翻译第一稿,在翻译的过程中译者与编辑随时进行交流,译稿完成后编辑进行校对,并与译者共同修改,修改完成后由主编进行最后审定。我本人并非翻译专业出身,但在参与《中华人文》的编辑工作伊始,就被这一过程中所出现的各种问题深深吸引。尽管知道翻译理论研究并非自己的专业,但我在 2014年还是忍不住写了一篇完全基于自己编辑实践的论文——《译者—编辑合作模式在中国文学外译中的实践——以毕飞宇三部短篇小说的英译为例》,由此开启了学术研究的新方向,并至今乐此不疲。目前《中华人文》正在着手建立翻译过程语料库,《文库》的翻译过程语料也将加入其中。语料库拟对所有研究翻译的学者开放,开展多角度的研究,丰富翻译研究的路径。翻译过程语料库

effectively Going Global, but is also truly being appreciated.

The present *Library* also aims to attract scholars' attention to the process of literary translation. As mentioned above, the translators of the *Library* are all sinologists whose mother tongue is English. At the same time, they collaborate with Chinese editors who are teachers from the School of Foreign Languages and Cultures at Nanjing Normal University, specializing in literature or translation. The basic collaboration process involves the translator finishing the first draft and communicating with the editor whenever questions arise. After the first draft is finished, the editor proofreads it, then revises it with the translator. After the revision is completed, the editor-in-chief checks and approves the final draft. I am not a translation major, but from the time I began my job as editor at *Chinese Arts & Letters*, I was drawn to the various challenges that arose during this process. Although I knew little about translation theory, I could not wait to write an article entirely based on my own editing experience, "The Translator-Editor Collaboration in Translating Chinese Literature—Three Short Stories by Bi Feiyu as Case Studies" in 2014. It has opened a new direction in my academic research, in which I have never lost interest. At present, *Chinese Arts & Letters* is setting up a Translation Process Corpus, and the materials in the translation process of the *Library* will be added to the Corpus as well. The Corpus will be open to all translation scholars to conduct studies from various perspectives and enrich the approaches to translation

体现了母语为英语的译者与母语为中文的编辑之间的充分交流：译者和编辑各自发挥自己的母语优势，在两种语言、两种文化之间互动交融，努力使译文既符合目标读者群的阅读习惯与审美趣味，又准确传达原文背后深刻的文化内涵。我们甚至可以设想，如果能将这种集中了翻译场域中人类智慧的翻译过程语料，以合适的方式对人工智能进行"投喂"，让人工智能进行深度学习，将来也许可以将语言的细微之处翻译出精妙的美感，真正突破人工智能在翻译水平方面的瓶颈。

尽管以上所提到的目标读者都相对专业，但我们仍然希望《文库》雅俗共赏，成为文学爱好者的枕边书。杨昊成教授曾对当代青年只看手机不看书的状况提出严厉的批评：他们"似乎更喜欢来自新媒体的碎片化阅读，严肃文学因此令人悲哀地受到轻视或藐视，被遗忘在图书馆的书架上，满是尘埃，仅成为少数书生的精神食粮"。他希望本文库能挽回一部分"迷途的羔羊"，让他们"回到传统的纸质阅读的正常轨道上来"。我觉得自己没有资格批评——尽管我已经不能算作是"当代青年"，但我看手机的

studies. The Translation Process Corpus showcases the communication between the translator who is a native speaker of English and the editor who is a native speaker of Chinese. They each exert their own mother tongue advantages, and interaction occurs between the two languages and cultures. They seek to make the translated text not only satisfy the target audience's reading habits and aesthetic preferences, but also convey the deepest cultural connotations of the original text. We may even imagine that if these materials crystalizing human intelligence in the translation field were "fed" in the proper way into an artificial intelligence and became deep-learning materials for AI, AI would one day translate every subtlety of the language with delicacy and beauty, breaking the bottleneck in AI translation.

Though, as mentioned earlier, the target audience of these works is relatively professional, we hope that the present *Library* will suit both refined and popular tastes and be put beside the pillows of all readers who are interested in literature. Professor Yang Haocheng once criticized young people today for being interested only in cellphones instead of books, saying, "So it is fragmented reading from the new media that college students seem to be enjoying today, and serious literature is woefully slighted or neglected, forgotten in the dust-covered shelves of the libraries, becoming the spiritual food for a minority of bookish souls." He hoped the *Library* would bring back some of "the lost lambs to the

频率已经远远超过了看纸质书的频率，应该也算是杨昊成教授所批评的"迷途的羔羊"之一。然而，我们还是希望《文库》能让大家稍稍改变一下习惯，每天花一点时间阅读纸质书，《文库》中的短篇小说也许就是最好的开始。本文库第一辑所译介的作家之一苏童曾说："短篇小说就像针对成年人的夜间故事，最好在灯下读，最好是每天入睡前读一篇，玩味三五分钟，或者被感动，或者会心一笑，或者怅怅然的，如有骨鲠在喉，如果读出这样的味道，说明这短暂的阅读时间没有浪费，培养这样的习惯使一天的生活终止于辉煌，多么好！"《文库》中不仅有精彩的短篇小说，更有相对照的英文版，相信读者一定会有双重的乐趣与收获。

文学评论家吴义勤、学者及翻译家许钧都从他们各自不同的视角出发，对本文库的出版表示了强有力的支持。两位都是他们各自领域的重要人物，他们的意见更增加了本文库的权威性。

《当代中国名家双语阅读文库》是开放性的，它会不断地出下

normal track of conventional paper book reading." I don't think I myself have the right to criticize young people today. Although I am not young, I read my cellphone much more frequently than I read paper books, which makes me one of "the lost lambs" criticized by Professor Yang Haocheng. But it is our hope that the *Library* will change our reading habits a little. If we plan to spend some time every day reading books, the short stories in the present *Library* are an ideal starting point. As Su Tong, one of the writers introduced in Volume One of the *Library*, once said, "Short stories are like bedtime stories for adults, preferably being read beside the lamp, one piece per night. They can be tasted for three or five minutes, moving, amusing, depressing, or overwhelming the reader. If you experience these feelings, it shows that this short period of time has not been wasted. A habit like this ensures that each day will end in magnificence. How wonderful it is!" The *Library* contains wonderful short stories in both Chinese and English, which, we believe, will surely bring readers double happiness and growth.

Literary critic Wu Yiqin, and academic and translator Xu Jun, have both voiced their strong support for this *Library*, each speaking from their different perspectives. Both of them are towering figures in their own fields, and their opinions add to the authority of the *Library*.

This *Library* is meant to be open ended, though it is set to be developed on a five-author basis, which includes five short stories

去。它以五位作家为一辑，每位作家为一卷，每卷包括五个短篇并附有一篇评论和一篇访谈，其中个别卷会略有变化。为了本文库的出版，各方面的人员做出了很多努力或给予了很大支持，其中包括我们杰出的翻译家、作家、评论家，《中华人文》和南京师范大学出版社的领导、编辑等，可以说这是一次令人快乐又组织有序的大合唱。历史会铭记我们的现任总指挥盛宁教授，会永远怀念首任主编杨昊成教授！

许诗焱

2020 年 9 月

alongside a critique and an interview for each author, with slight variations in each issue. Various people have contributed their effort and lent their support to the publication of the *Library,* including our terrific translators, authors, critics, editors from *Chinese Arts & Letters* and Nanjing Normal University Press, and the Press's leadership, so you may say it's a joyful, well-orchestrated tutti. History will remember our current conductor, Professor Sheng Ning, and will cherish our memory to Professor Yang Haocheng as our first editor-in-chief.

Xu Shiyan

September, 2020

目 录

Contents

土　炕

这大娘住在陕北羊儿沟，西离县城八十里，东离锁关镇三十里。她一生没去过县城，想不来城墙是怎么个厚法；锁关镇去过四次，一满去赶庙会，回来脚疼了几天。她恨过她娘，给她缠了脚；又发誓来世再不做女人了，不能英武武地

The Brick Bed

Translated by Denis Mair

She was a matron who lived in Yang'ergou in north Shaanxi Province, eighty *li* to the east of the county seat and thirty *li* to the west of Suoguan Town. In her whole life she never went to the county seat—so she had no idea how thick the ramparts could be—and only four times to Suoguan Town. She visited the temple fair all these four times, but after coming home her feet would ache for days. She had once hated her mother for binding her feet as a child; what is more, she

走州过县。

　　她娘家是关中人，十九岁上，一个亲戚做媒，将她嫁到这里。丈夫姓王，比她小了三岁，小猴猴个头。她当时很不悦意，哭了一场，但爹娘用了人家的钱，拗不过，只好去王家炕上做媳妇。过门的那天，丈夫用毛驴接的她，四个唢呐吹天吹地，村子里的人都来看热闹，她吓得伏在驴背上，不敢抬头。晚上闹了新房，窑门关了，剩下她和小猴猴，她想起她娘，又哭了；丈夫也不敢动她。第三天半夜，小猴猴爬过来，叫她"婆姨"，她说："谁是你婆姨，叫姐！"丈夫叫了一句"姐"，她才给他了个笑脸。

　　做了媳妇，滋味和做姑娘大不一样。丈夫虽然不能遮风挡雨，但对她尽心儿恩爱，她也就作罢了。他拉骡子去

vowed that in the next life she would not be born as a woman, unable to travel boldly across the land.

Her birth family had lived on the central Shaanxi Plain, but at age 19 a relative had acted as a go-between and married her off to a family here. Her husband's surname was Wang; he was three years her junior and monkey-like in stature. With a bout of crying she made her unwillingness known, but her parents had already accepted the Wangs' money, so her protests were futile: she had no choice but to climb onto Wang's bed and become a wife. On the day set for receiving the bride, her husband came to pick her up on a donkey. Four *suona* players tootled and filled the air with blaring notes as villagers lined the road to view the festivities. She timidly clutched the donkey's back, not daring to look up. That evening, after the groom's friends finished the horseplay in the nuptial chamber, the door of the cave-house was closed behind them, leaving her alone with Little Monkey. Pangs of separation from her mother triggered another fit of sobbing, so her husband dared not touch her that night. On the third night, Little Monkey crawled across the bed to her and addressed her "Wifie." She said, "I am not your Wifie. Call me 'Sister'!" Her husband called her Sister, and only then did she give him a smile.

Being a wife felt quite different from being an unmarried girl. Her husband could not shield her from rain and wind, but he was devoted and affectionate, so she gave in. He sometimes led a string of pack mules to Dingbian, hauling salt for one or

定边驮盐，一走一月两月，家里她里外忙活：冬种麦子，夏播糜谷；空闲下来，就拿了针线在村里串门。慢慢，倒觉得这地方不错，尤其是那土炕，在关中没有见过，她就感兴趣了。

土炕很大，长一丈二寸，宽六尺零五，占了整整后半个窑。窑窗下是灶台，灶口是个深坑，炭填进去，既烧饭，又从脚地下的火道里通到炕上，冬天里，满窑都显得暖和。但她不习惯这么大的炕。丈夫出门后，她一个人裹着被子，夜里睡得满炕滚，倒却乐得笑了几次。她提议把炕盘小，丈夫不同意，说将来要生儿育女，这炕上十个八个都能睡下；她听后飞红了脸。半夜起来解溲，她总想：真有七个八个儿女了，那炕下的鞋子会一摆一长溜呢，就又噗噗地笑。

two months each time, during which she kept busy with indoor and outdoor work at home: in the winter she planted wheat; in the summer she sowed millet. If she had free time she would visit neighbors chattering while doing some needlework. As time went by she came around to the view that this place was not bad, especially that heated brick bed. She had never seen a bed like that on the central Shaanxi Plain, so she found it intriguing.

The brick bed was big, measuring approximately three and a half meters in length and two and a quarter meters in width. It took up half of the whole cave-house. Beneath the cave's front window was a stove that had a deep cavity on top where charcoal was added. The fire was used for cooking meals, and it was connected to the brick bed by a duct underfoot. In winter the cave-house stayed warm, but she was not used to such a big bed. The first time her husband went away, she wrapped herself in a big cover and had the whole bed to herself at night. She rolled this way and that during the night, making herself chuckle a few times. She suggested that he re-do the brickwork to make the bed smaller, but he didn't agree, claiming that when they had children in the future, the bed would be able to sleep eight or ten people. Hearing him say this made her face blush. Getting up at night to use the chamber-pot, she would always think: if we really do have seven or eight kids, their shoes will make a long row beneath the bed. That made her chuckle again.

土炕成了她的天地，她在上边纺线、纳鞋帮；在炕上摊开包袱，一有空闲，就翻弄那些各色布头、丝线；晚上在上边和丈夫说悄悄话。她想：男人家走州过县，女人家就是要守住这块土炕。她便尽心儿打扮：单子不许折一个皱，炕沿不能沾半星尘。只是不习惯在上边坐着吃饭，说是委屈不了那腿儿。

过了三年，她却一个儿女也没有生养下来。丈夫虽然心里苦恼，对她也不敢说出重话。她背着人哭了一场，觉得有了亏，便不再对他要强；丈夫反倒更爱怜她。

这时候，中央红军已到了延安，解放了西北边儿几个县，可胡宗南常来侵犯，这地面就成了拉锯区：一会白的过来，一会红的过；日月不安宁起来。这一天，东南方向枪响了一个时辰，村里人都躲在家里不敢出门。天一黑，她就关门睡觉，窑畔上"咯"地响了一下，便有什么落在院子里

The brick bed became her personal domain: she sat on it while spinning yarn and sewing cloth shoes; on its broad surface she spread her bundle of possessions; in her idle time she would sort through colorful silk threads and pieces of cloth. In the evening, she and her husband would murmur confidences there. She thought: a man makes his way freely through the outside world; a woman should watch over this brick bed. She did her best to make it look nice, spreading the covers without a wrinkle and not letting a speck of dust settle along its base. Even so she could not get in the habit of eating on the bed, saying that was hard on her legs.

Three years later she still hadn't given birth, not even to a daughter. Although her husband was vexed, he could not bring himself to speak harshly to her. She went off by herself and cried miserably over her cruel fate. After that, feeling a little guilty, she never tried to get the upper hand over her husband, and he ended up showing more love and affection for her.

By this time the Central Red Army had arrived at Yan'an after the Long March and had liberated several counties along the northwest border. Even so, General Hu Zongnan's army often made forays, so a see-saw conflict unfolded across this piece of terrain. During those unquiet times, the Whites would come, and then the Reds would drive them away. That day, gunfire was heard for two hours, coming from the southeast, so the villagers stayed behind closed doors. As darkness fell

了。出来看时，是一个女八路。女八路说：前边战斗很残酷，队伍冲散了，自己掉了队，要求进窑来歇歇。她吓了一跳，但还是让女八路进了窑。

这女八路脸黄黄的，腰身很笨，她一眼看出有着身孕，就越发怜惜起来，做汤烧水，让坐在土炕上。女八路看着他们善良，很是感激，但见只有这一孔窑洞，又见是才成亲的小两口，便觉得住着不便，丈夫也没了主意。她说：

"快上炕，咱们陕北，就是这风俗，家里人几辈睡一个炕哩。"

她让女八路睡在西边，让丈夫睡在东边，她在中间躺下，作了界墙。那女八路还是不肯睡下。她只好推醒丈夫，让他睡到灶口前的脚地，说只许面朝外。丈夫一夜没敢翻身。

她夜里悄悄问女八路：

"你当了几年兵？"

and they barred the door, preparing to sleep, they heard the thud of something landing in the yard outside the cave. Going out for a look, they found a female soldier of the Eighth Route Army. She told them that her unit had scattered in the face of a fierce onslaught, and she had gotten separated from her squad. She asked to come inside the cave and rest. This gave the wife a fright, but she let the female soldier come inside.

The soldier's face was a waxy yellow, and her protuberant torso moved stiffly. The wife could tell at a glance that the female soldier was pregnant, which made her all the more solicitous. She boiled water and told the female soldier to sit on the bed. Seeing the couple's kindness, the female soldier was quite grateful, but after all they were a newly married couple occupying a single cave, so staying there did not seem convenient. The husband was indecisive, but the wife said, "Get up on the bed. This is our custom here in North Shaanxi—people under the same roof sleep on the same *brick bed*."

She told the female soldier to sleep on the west side and her husband to sleep on the east, with herself in the middle as a barrier. Still the female soldier would not go to sleep. The wife had no choice but to rouse her husband and make him stretch out on the ground in front of the stove, saying he was only allowed to face outward. Her husband laid there all night without daring to turn over.

The Brick Bed

土炕

"一年八个月了。"

"打死过人吗?"

"用枪瞄了一个胡儿子,倒下没有起来,我没去看死了
没死。"

"你真行,我杀鸡手都颤哩。"

"逼出来的,我爹娘是被胡儿子用刺刀挑死的,族里把
我卖给一家当童养媳,我偷跑的。"

她心里动了一下,不自觉看了一眼她的猴猴丈夫。

"现在丈夫在哪?"

"在延安。不知这阵在哪儿打仗。"

"孩子几个月了?"

"七个半月了。"

"真作孽,还敢这么凶跑?"

"我真后悔怀上了,恨不得一把抓了出来!"

第二天,女八路要走,她留住了,说那太危险,路上生

At night she asked the female soldier in a hushed tone:
"How many years have you been a soldier?"

"One year and eight months."

"Have you killed anyone?"

"I had a Hu's soldier in my sights and pulled the trigger. He fell down and didn't get up, but I didn't stick around to see if he was dead."

"You really have what it takes. My hands get quivery just from killing a chicken."

"It was forced upon me. My father and mother were bayoneted by the Hu's army; then I was sold by my clan to another family as a child bride, but I ran away."

She felt a twitch in her heart and unconsciously directed a look at her husband.

"Where is your husband now?"

"He is in Yan'an. Right now he may be off somewhere fighting a battle."

"How far along is your pregnancy?"

"Seven-and-a-half months."

"Good grief. It's horrible to be running about in your condition."

"I really regret getting pregnant. If only I could get it ripped out of me!"

The next day, the female soldier got ready to go. The wife held her back, saying it would be terrible if the birth

养下来，如何了得？女八路就住下来。她也知道了这女八路叫龚娟，是个宣传员。

这天夜里，龚娟肚子果然就疼起来，一扭一扭地疼。她赶忙在灶口的脚地推醒了丈夫，让他出去抱了一捆麦草进来，就把他关在窑外了。两个人都没有生过娃，心慌手抖的，忙乱了几个时辰，孩子总算落了草。她用灰垫了脚地的血水，开门把丈夫叫进来，烧饭烧炕，又拿了一溜红布，挂在窑门栓子上，说是避邪。

孩子是个女的，瘦得像只猫儿，她们就叫猫猫，龚娟喜欢，她两口也是喜欢，终日关了窑门，不透风声出去。过了十天，龚娟在土炕上坐不住了，要出门去追部队。临走，留下猫猫，给她跪下说：

"大姐，我不能再呆了，这孩子带不走，就托付了你，权当你救了一命。要是个好的，你抚养长大，就是你的女儿，要是有个不好，你把她埋了，我一辈子都记着你的

happened along the way. So the female soldier agreed to stay in the cave. The wife found out the woman's name—it was Gong Juan, and she was a propaganda staffer.

That night, Gong Juan felt pain in her belly, and the pain began coming in spasms. The wife roused her husband from his slumber at the base of the bed, telling him to bring in a bundle of straw. Then she locked him outside the cave. Neither of the women had dealt with a birth before, so they fumbled about with trembling hands. After an ordeal of almost ten hours, the child finally came into the world onto the straw. The wife strewed ashes over the bloodied foot-platform, then called her husband in. She cooked a meal and heated the bed, then hung a red streamer in the doorway, saying it would ward off ill fortune.

The child was a girl, as skinny as a cat, so they called her Kitty. Gong Juan was delighted with her, and so were the husband and wife. They kept the cave door closed all day, not letting any word of the child slip out. After ten days of sitting on the brick bed, Gong Juan grew restless, wanting to go and find her squad. Before leaving she set Kitty on the bed and knelt in front of the wife, saying: "Elder-Sister, I cannot stay any longer. I can't take this child with me, so I'm leaving her in your care. Let's just say you will be her lifesaver. If she turns out well, then you can raise her up and have her for a daughter. If something is wrong with her, then bury her.

恩情。"

她扶起了龚娟，流着眼泪说：

"龚妹子，你放心走吧，我虽是人穷，良心还没坏，你的孩子就是我的孩子，我一定好好抚养。等有了好日子，我等着你来接了她去。"

龚娟磕了几个头，抱着孩子又亲又哭，末了，就走了。

她开始在这土炕上养着猫猫长大。她没有奶，孩子饿得蛮哭，她让丈夫去卖了炕上一条新被子，买回来一头奶羊，天天给孩子挤着吃。她在外边放风，说是自己不生养，在路上捡到这个孩子的，村里人也没有生疑。以后自己也真的没生下儿女，两年过去，也不见那龚娟来接女儿，只道是牺牲了，就越发疼这猫猫。

猫猫长到三岁，猴猴丈夫得了痨病，没救得过来，没了。她哭了一场，不去改嫁，从此做了寡妇。那年她刚刚二

Either way, I'll owe you a lifelong debt for your kindness."

The wife helped Gong Juan to her feet and said tearfully: "Sister Gong, you can go with your mind at ease. Though I live in a poor household, my conscience is still intact. Your child is my child; I will bring it up as best I can. When peaceful days come again, I'll wait for you to come and get her back."

Gong Juan prostrated herself before the wife, touching her forehead to the floor several times. She held the child, kissing it and sobbing. When she had cried enough, she left.

On this brick bed the wife began to raise the child Kitty. She had no milk and the child was squalling with hunger. She told her husband to sell the new quilt from their bed, with which he bought a milch goat. Each day they milked the goat to feed the child. She let out word that she had picked up a foundling beside the road and, being unable to conceive a child herself, she had decided to raise it. No one in the village doubted her. Two years passed: she still did not bear a child of her own. Gong Juan still did not come for the child, which led the wife to believe that she had fallen in battle. It also made the wife's affection for the child grow all the stronger.

When Kitty was three years old, the monkeyish husband contracted tuberculosis. Her attempts to nurse him through the fever failed, and he passed away. She had a good long cry, and after that she would not remarry. She became a widow at

十六岁。

做了寡妇，日月就更加艰难。她短了言语，轻易不大出门，偶尔窑外跑来几只野猫野狗的，要么撵出去，要么关了门。四邻八舍，谁也说不出个闲话来。

她心性高强，天大的难处，只藏在肚里，人面前不露一点恓惶。猫猫的衣服，虽然不十分鲜亮，但绝对干净。家里一切开支全靠她纺线，她线纺得又快又好，别人每天纺一斤六两，她纺二斤一两，拿到集上去卖，要比别人多卖出好多价。

这年春天，西北方面完全解放了，村子里纺线的人多起来，政府也收购棉线、毛线。她从此就不去集上卖高价了，一律卖给政府。干部表扬她，她公布了猫猫的身世，说：孩子的娘是八路军，人家能拿枪打敌人，她要多纺些线，才配得起是猫猫的养母。村上就选她和一个叫吴二章的到延安去

the age of twenty-six.

As a widow times were even harder than before. She became a woman of few words, and she did not lightly go out her gate. At times wild dogs or feral cats would come near; she would chase them out of the cave and close the door. Among her neighbors there were no gossips about her.

She was stoical, with high self-esteem, able to hide the most grievous hardships within herself, and never showing the slightest anxiety in front of others. Although Kitty's clothes were somewhat drab, they were absolutely clean. For all household expenses she relied on her spinning work. She spun thread and yarn, rapidly and neatly: other people could only spin one *jin* six *liang* per day, but she could spin two *jin* one *liang*. The thread she spun brought a better price than the thread spun by others.

In spring of that year the Northwest was thoroughly liberated, and more people in the village were spinning thread than before. The government began purchasing cotton thread and wool yarn. From then on she never sold her thread for a high price in the market; she reserved it to sell to the government. When the local cadres praised her at an assembly, she announced Kitty's parentage, saying: "The child's mother was an enlisted woman in the Eighth Route Army, a woman who went up against the enemy with gun in hand. I have to spin as much thread as I can to be a worthy foster mother for

开劳模会，但她终是没去，觉得妇道人家，走不到人前去，评不评模范，反正她是要多纺线的。结果吴二章当了模范，后来跟部队到山西去作战，立了功劳，新中国成立后在西安城里做了干部。她依然还住在羊儿沟，黑天白日在土炕上纺棉花。

新中国成立后，猫猫长大了，她供着去读小学。猫猫学习好，她脸上有光，夜里搂着在土炕上睡，说：

"爱我不?"

"爱。"

"长大养活我不?"

"养活。"

她把猫猫搂得紧紧的。

可是这年秋天，她们正在院子里打枣儿，听见车响，一抬头，沟畔的路上，嘟嘟地开来了一辆小车，跳下一伙城里的人，一直向她家窑门走来。她感到新奇，不知道这是些什

Kitty." The village selected her and a man named Wu Erzhang to take part in a "Model Worker Assembly" in Yan'an, but ultimately she did not go. She felt that being a woman was her lot in life, and it wouldn't be fitting to show off in front of many people. Whether or not she was recognized as a model worker, she would try to spin more thread anyway. As for Wu Erzhang, having been named a model worker he was recruited to fight in Shanxi. He won a combat medal, and after the founding of New China in 1949 served as a cadre in Xi'an. Meanwhile she went on living in Yang'ergou, spinning cotton thread night and day on her brick bed.

After the founding of New China, Kitty grew to girlhood. The woman paid for Kitty's schooling, and Kitty's excellence as a student reflected well on her. Lying on the brick bed arm-in-arm with Kitty she said, "Do you love me?"

"Yes."

"When you grow up will you support me?"

"Yes, I will."

She hugged Kitty tightly.

But that fall as she stood in her courtyard knocking down jujubes with a long pole, she heard an automobile engine. Looking up she saw a sedan pulling up at the edge of the road. A group of city folks tumbled out of the car and came walking straight toward her cave-house. It was quite an unusual sight, and she had no idea who the people were. She was telling Kitty

The Brick Bed

土炕

么人，正教猫猫说那是小汽车，那伙人就进了院。一位壮年妇女看着她，叫了一声"大姐!"就哭出声来了。她莫名其妙。那女的说她是龚娟，她"噢"地叫了一声，说"你还活着!"就呜呜咽咽起来了。

这天夜里，她们说了一夜话，龚娟告诉她，当时从这里出去，找着了部队，就开到前线去了，后来又去了新疆，再没有回到陕北。新中国成立后，打问了几次，又没有找到，前一个月才有了消息。

"大姐，真苦了你，这么多年，一把屎一把尿把孩子拉扯这么大，我真不知道怎么感激你呢! 现在革命成功了，我真不忍心带了她去，留下你一个人在这里；你还是一块进城去吧，我永远叫你姐姐，猫猫也永远叫你是娘。"

她笑笑，说她有什么功劳，要到城里去? 就劝说猫猫认了亲娘，猫猫不去，她倒变了脸。

第二天，她喜喜欢欢打发龚娟母女走了。车一拐过山

that it was called an "automobile" when the group walked into her yard. Among them, a city woman in her late thirties spoke the greeting "Big Sister," then burst out crying. It was baffling at first, until the woman identified herself as Gong Juan "*Oh*, you're still alive!" she exclaimed and began sobbing too.

That night they stayed up talking until dawn. Gong Juan told how she had gone out from the cave and found her unit. Before long they advanced to the front line. After that she was sent to Xinjiang, and she never made it back to northern Shaanxi. After the founding of New China, she tried to make inquiries, but no answer came. The news had come to her only a month ago.

"Big Sister, I know it hasn't been easy for you. You wiped her butt and kept her well-fed through babyhood, so she could grow into a girl. Really, I don't know how to show my gratitude. Now the revolution has succeeded. I can hardly bring myself to take her away and leave you here alone. I'll tell you what, you can come to the city with us. I will always call you Older Sister, and Kitty will always call you Mother."

The village woman laughed, saying she had done nothing to be worthy of going to the city. She urged Kitty to recognize the city woman as birth-mother. At first Kitty didn't want to go to the city, so the village woman put on a stern face.

The next day she smilingly saw off the girl and Gong

弯,她却扑腾在路上,哭得哇哇地伤心。

从此,她有了一门亲戚在西安城里,三天两头托人给她们写信。母女俩也给她回信,时常还捎来钱,十元、八元。她舍不得花,买些山货特产又寄去。她们让她去城里游游,她信上应着,却一直没有动身。

猫猫在城里读完高中,龚娟便病故了。不久猫猫参加了工作,信便来得少了,先是两个月一封,后是半年一封,信又越写越短,最后竟再没有来过一句话了。

她却老是盼着,差不多过两天就去邮电所打问。村里人瞧她可怜,说:

"听说猫猫当了局长了。"

"是吗?"

"她真没良心,当了官把你忘了!"

"可不敢说那话!当了领导事忙嘛。"

Juan, but when the car was out of sight she fell over on the road and wailed wretchedly.

Now that she had a relative in Xi'an City, every few days she would ask someone to write a letter for her, and she received answering letters from the mother and daughter. She occasionally received small sums of money from them, eight or ten *yuan* at a time. She couldn't bear to spend it on herself, so she bought local produce and mailed it. They invited her to make a trip to the city, just for fun. In one letter she agreed to go, but she never got around to it.

After Kitty graduated from middle school, Gong Juan contracted an illness and died. Not long after that, Kitty began a full-time job, and fewer letters came. First there was one letter every two months, but later once in half a year. The letters that did come were shorter and shorter, and eventually no word came at all.

Even so she kept waiting expectantly. Every third day or so she inquired at the post office. People in the village felt sorry for her and said, "We've heard that Kitty was promoted to bureau chief."

"Is that so?"

"I wonder if she has a conscience. Now that she's an official, she forgets you!"

"That is no way to talk. Serving as a leader keeps her busy."

The Brick Bed

土炕

"忙总不能忘了你。你把她抚养大了，你能不让她养活？"

"如果是为了如今养活我才收养她，那我成什么人啦！"

这话，是说给别人的，也是说给自己的。于是她就想开了，也不在心里埋怨猫猫。她只是纺她的棉花，春纺到夏，夏纺到冬，挣些钱，一半添了新衣，一半买了粮食。谁要再提说猫猫的事，她就抖着新衣，敲着碗沿说：

"说那话多没出息，我又不是七老八十了，过不去了？！"

只是那大炕，睡起来觉得太硬，一年四季上边铺了麦草。有人让打了那炕，给她盘个小的。她不，说她什么都可以丢下心，就是不舍这土炕，夜里睡在上边，可以做好多梦，梦见她那猴猴丈夫，也梦猫猫母女。

那几年里，省上、县上的干部经常下乡，男的来，女的也来。村里就把女干部派在她炕上来睡。她很乐意，十

"Even if she's busy it's not right to forget you. You raised her. I think she owes it to you to provide for you. "

"If I raised her back then just so she would support me now, what kind of person would I be?"

She said this for other people to hear, but also for herself to hear. Thus she was able to take a broad view and didn't hold anything against Kitty. She just kept spinning cotton yarn; she spun from spring to summer and then from summer to winter. Half of the money she earned went for new clothes and half went for staple foods. If anyone broached the subject of Kitty, she would smooth her new jacket and tap the edge of her bowl, saying, "Talking about that doesn't get us anywhere. I'm not an old lady in my seventies or eighties; I'm getting by, aren't I?"

Yet the big brick bed was mighty hard to sleep on, so she put down padding of straw all through the year. People advised her to take out the bed and have a smaller one made. She wouldn't do it. She said that she could let go of everything else, but not that brick bed. Sleeping on that brick bed, she could have plenty of dreams—about her monkeyish husband or about Kitty and her mother.

During those years, cadres from county and provincial governments were frequently sent down to the countryside. Many of them were men, but women also came. When female cadres came, the village would arrange for them to sleep on the

个八个都让挤在土炕上。她睡得迟，挑灯看她们每一张漂

亮的脸，一看见那炕下的鞋，就想起当年和丈夫说的话，

没笑出声来，却去把各色各式的鞋放得整整齐齐。早上，

女干部刷牙，她也用盐水漱口，人老了，牙齿不齐，但白

得像玉。

到她六十岁上，闹起"文化大革命"，到她炕上来睡的

女干部就少了。她常常念叨她们，全记着她们的名字。但在

人面前，她从来没有提说过猫猫。只是每年枣子红了，她在

心里就想起来，很是难过一个时间。

几年过去，社会虽安宁不下来，却从北京、南京、西宁

来了好多学生，是插队落户的。她悄悄打问过猫猫，有的稍

有知道，说猫猫是走资派，在西安城里曾剃了光头游街。她

听了，不禁伤了心，说她看着猫猫长大，从没动过一个指

woman's brick bed. She was glad to let eight or ten of them squeeze onto the brick bed. She stayed up later than them, and as she held the lamp she could see a line of pretty faces. Looking down she saw their shoes placed along the base of the bed, which reminded her of a conversation with her husband years before. She held back a laugh as she arranged the varicolored shoes in a neat row. In the morning the female cadres brushed their teeth while she rinsed her mouth with salt water. Her teeth were not as straight as before but were still white like jade.

Around the time she turned sixty, the "Cultural Revolution" broke out, and fewer female cadres came to sleep on her brick bed. She often thought of them and could remember all their names. Yet she never spoke of Kitty in front of them. When the jujubes in her yard turned ripe and red, she would sometimes think of Kitty, deep in her heart, and feel sad for a spell.

A couple of years passed, and peace was not yet restored in society, when groups of students started coming to the countryside from Beijing, Nanjing and Xining. They had to join production brigades and settle down in the village. She discretely inquired about Kitty. Some of the students knew about Kitty: they said she had been branded as a "capitalist roader" and had been paraded through the streets with her head shaven. Hearing this made the woman's heart ache: while caring for

头，如何受得下那份罪？

忽有一日，邮电所送来一封信，她慌得厉害，不知道谁会给她来信，让人代念了，才知是猫猫的，信上写得更可怜，说她犯了错误，现在五七干校改造；说她已有三个孩子，受人歧视，准备要赶到边远的地方去下乡，她不放心，想让大女儿落户到羊儿沟，让养母护着；说她这些年忘了本，没给养母来信，害怕养母不愿意。

她听了，眼泪又流下来，连忙让人写了回信。信上说：

"让来吧，让来吧！我怎么不愿意呢？孩子有了难处，到这儿了，就住在我家，炕还是那老土炕，我也不孤单，谁也不敢欺负孩子的，快让来吧！"

猫猫的大女儿不久就来了。这孩子十六岁，叫秀秀，和猫猫眉眼儿似像。一见面，秀秀叫她一声："奶！"她叫着猫

Kitty as a child she had never laid a finger on the girl. How could Kitty bear such mistreatment?

Suddenly one day the postman brought a letter. This gave the woman a terrible start, because she did not know who would write to her. Only when it was read to her did she know it was from Kitty. It was a heartbreaking letter that told how Kitty had committed errors and was now being reformed at a cadre education farm. Kitty already had three children of her own, and people were prejudiced against them. Preparations were underway to send the children to a remote area. Kitty was worried about them and was hoping to send her oldest daughter to live in Yang'ergou under the woman's care. Kitty admitted to forgetting her roots and not keeping in touch with her own foster mother, so she feared the woman would not be willing.

The woman's tears poured down as she heard the letter being read. She quickly asked someone to write a return letter, which went as follows:

"Let her come! Let her come! Why should I be unwilling? Since the child has difficulties, have her come here and she can live in my place. I still have that big brick bed. The girl will keep me company, and nobody will dare to mistreat her. Let her come soon!"

Before long Kitty's oldest daughter arrived, a sixteen-year-old girl named Xiuxiu, with eyes that looked much like Kitty's. At first sight Xiuxiu called the woman "Grandma."

The Brick Bed

土炕

猫的名字，搂着就哭了。

从此，土炕上睡了秀秀，夜夜她给孩子讲猫猫小时候的事，婆孙俩就笑一笑。秀秀也讲这几年家里的遭遇，她抹一阵眼泪，成半夜睡不下觉。

秀秀什么也不会做，她教着认庄稼、拿锄、洗衣服，叮咛人品要正，要舍得出力。秀秀也乖，样样听她的，收工回来，见她做好了饭，总要第一碗让她先吃，她乐得脚颤手抖。过了冬天，秀秀来了例假，吓得不知道怎么办，她经管着，讲了好多事情，不让秀秀动冷水，不让干重活。秀秀反应大，身子不舒服，想起娘，夜里老哭，她就彻夜坐着劝说。村里人见她护着秀秀，谁也不敢作践。

待了两年，秀秀越发变成个大姑娘，肩膀宽了，胸脯高

The woman inadvertently called out "Kitty" and embraced her tearfully.

So then Xiuxiu was there with her. Lying in bed each night, she told Xiuxiu stories about Kitty's childhood which provoked both into a chuckle at times. Xiuxiu for her part spoke of what her family had gone through for the past few years. Xiuxiu's story reduced her to tears and kept her awake half the night.

Xiuxiu did not know how to do anything. The woman taught her to recognize food crops, use a hoe and wash clothes. She admonished the girl to be upright in character and not to shrink from doing hard work. Xiuxiu was a well-behaved girl and did as she was told. Coming home from work and seeing that the woman had supper ready, Xiuxiu would scoop the first portion into the woman's bowl. The woman's hands trembled with joy to see such thoughtfulness. At winter's end Xiuxiu began having her monthly periods. At first Xiuxiu was scared and didn't know what to do. The woman took her in hand and gave her pointers, telling her not to touch cold water and not to do heavy work. One night menstrual cramps and separation from her mother caused Xiuxiu to lie awake crying. The woman stayed up all night urging Xiuxiu to look at the bright side. Seeing that the woman was so protective of Xiuxiu, no one in the village dared to treat the girl harshly.

After a stay of two years, Xiuxiu had grown into an

The Brick Bed
土炕

高挺起来，出脱得很漂亮。其中回了三次西安，猫猫让捎回了好多衣服给她。

她问秀秀：

"乡里好？城里好？"

"乡里好。"

"将来你娘在城里住着难受了，让她也来住。"

"那该是好，我就一辈子守着奶奶。"

"那我以后就给你招个女婿上门吧。"

"可往哪儿住呀？"

"这么大个土炕，还没你小两口睡吗？"

"嘻嘻……"秀秀脸红得像朵花。

过了春天，秀秀又进城去了，她让给猫猫捎话，说要愿意到乡下，全家都可来住在她家，看谁还敢剃了头发游街？秀秀回去后，却一个月没有回来。她很焦急，担心是在路上

attractive young woman with broad shoulders and firm, pert breasts. During that period Xiuxiu made three short visits to Xi'an, and each time Kitty would send along clothes to give the woman.

The woman asked Xiuxiu, "Which do you like more, the countryside or the city?"

"I like the countryside."

"In the future if your mother gets tired of living in the city, have her come here to live."

"That would be nice. I would watch over you all my life."

"Then someday we'll find a son-in-law who's willing to marry into our household."

"But where would he live?"

"There's plenty of room for a young couple to sleep on such a large bed."

"Hee hee..." Xiuxiu's blushing face looked like a flower.

At the end of spring Xiuxiu went back to the city. The woman asked Xiuxiu to relay a message to Kitty, saying Kitty's whole family could come to the village and live in the countryside. No one in the village would dare to shave Kitty's head and parade her on the streets. A month passed after Xiuxiu left, but still she did not come back. The woman was anxious, fearing that something had happened to Xiuxiu along

出了事，就拍电报去城里。不久，信回来了。

信是秀秀写的，说回到城里，正赶上娘平了反，又恢复了局长职务。便要让她们在乡下的姐妹都调回城。

"可我还想回羊儿沟，我舍不得离开你。"秀秀在信上写道，"我睡惯了热土炕，睡在楼上的沙发床上，反倒睡不着呢。"

她一颗心放了下去，又一颗心提了上来，怕秀秀万一不能回来。村里人都在说："秀秀不会回来了，人家一定是有了工作，还来乡下受苦吗?"

"秀秀说要回来的，她说我这土炕好呢。"她总是这么说。

但是，秀秀到底没有回来，信倒来了四封，果然是工作了，信上尽是感激话，说永生永世不会忘了她的恩情，为了报答老人，就将那一套铺盖、衣物、用品，都留给她。只要

the way, so she sent a cable to the city. Before long a letter came in return.

The letter was from Xiuxiu, saying that her mother had been vindicated and had regained her post as bureau chief. Now they would be able to have Xiuxiu's sent-down sisters transferred back to the city.

"But I still want to return to Yang'ergou," continued Xiuxiu's letter. "I don't feel right leaving you, and I'm used to sleeping on that heated brick bed. I can't get to sleep on a thick mattress, in an upstairs room, but I can't get to sleep."

The woman was greatly relieved, but at the same time was on pins and needles. She worried that if something might prevent Xiuxiu from coming. All the villagers were saying, "Xiuxiu won't be coming back. She probably found a job in the city, so it's not likely she'd be back and suffer here." Each time the woman would reply, "Xiuxiu says she'll come back. She says the brick bed suits her."

As it turned out, Xiuxiu did not come back, but she did send four letters. Sure enough, she had gotten a job. The letters were brimming with words of gratitude, saying she would remember the woman's kindness all her life. To make recompense, she insisted on leaving her bedding, clothes and personal articles for her foster grandmother. She only requested

The Brick Bed
土炕

求把户口关系代办一下，转进城就是了。

她听了，没有言语。当天下午，踮着小脚去办了户口，连夜邮寄去了。回来睡在炕上，只觉得炕大、炕空，天明时，浑身发烧，睡倒不起了。

这一病，睡了十五天，等下了土炕，人老了许多，头发全白了，棉花也没力气去纺，只能一天做三顿饭，饭也吃得寡味。秀秀以后也没有来信，村里人做了研究，就"五保"了她。

她言语越发少起来，更是不大出门，终日坐在土炕上。土炕是太大了，她觉得占了地方，实在不合算。那灶台也大，一个人全然用不着那么大个锅。那窑墙上的架板上，米面盆儿，油盐罐儿，也放得不是个地方。她有心去拾掇，没有力气，就眯着眼，像是睡觉，其实醒着，醒得又不清白，黑天白日都是这样了。

that the woman help with the procedure for transferring household registry to the city.

She listened wordlessly as the letter was read to her. That afternoon she hobbled about taking care of the household registry papers, then posted them before the evening mail pickup. She went home and laid down on the *bed* but could only feel its big emptiness. At daybreak she felt feverish all over and couldn't even rise.

She was laid up with this illness for fifteen days. When it was over she got down from the bed, white-haired and much older-looking. She had no strength to spin cotton thread. She managed to cook meals for herself, but the food had lost its savor. Xiuxiu did not write any letters after that. People in the village looked into the matter and marked the woman out for providing basic welfare benefits for the rest of her life.

She became a woman of even fewer words and went out less than before. All day long she just sat on the brick bed. The brick bed was too long—she felt it took up too much space and wasn't good for anything. The stove was also too large, and a single person did not need such a large wok. On the shelves mounted against the wall, crocks and food canisters and plates were all in a jumble. She lacked the enthusiasm and energy to straighten them up, even if she had a mind to, so she just faced them with lowered eyelids. She seemed to doze during waking hours—awake but not very clear-minded. Night and day she was in this state.

眼睛不甚济事，耳朵却还灵，听院里风响，是一片树叶又在旋了。接着，窑畔上有了脚步声，一直响到窑门口。她叫一声："吴三章！"门帘一挑，进来的果然是吴三章。

吴三章是当年吴二章的弟弟。"文化大革命"中，吴二章受了批斗，后来折磨死了，如今平了反，坟迁埋在城里烈士陵园，吴三章便成了烈属，有了优待，日子十分滋润，近来常来串门。

"嫂子，你真可怜，秀秀她们如今平了反，又是做官，你怎么还是这样？"

她总是笑笑。

"你为什么不向她们要吗？"

"我'五保'了，我还要什么呀？"

"天底下还有这没良心的，有难了就记着了你，好过了便全忘记。"

Her vision blurred but her hearing was still sharp, able to hear the wind blow down a single leaf in the courtyard. Then she heard footsteps along the hill's edge, heading for the cave mouth. She called out, "Is that you, Wu Sanzhang?" A hand lifted the curtain in the doorway: sure enough the one who entered was Wu Sanzhang.

Wu Sanzhang was the younger brother of Wu Erzhang, with whom she could have shared the "model worker" honors years ago. Erzhang had been a target of persecution during the Great Cultural Revolution and had died of the torments he suffered. Recently he had been vindicated posthumously, and his grave had been moved to a martyr's cemetery in the city. Thus his younger brother Sanzhang had gotten preferential treatment as a martyr's relative, so he could live comfortably. Recently he had been coming to look in on her.

"I really pity you, Big Sister. Now that Xiuxiu's mother has been vindicated and restored to her post, I don't see why you're still in such a fix. Why don't you ask them for some help?"

She just chuckled when he talked like that. "I'm getting basic benefits. What is there to ask for?"

"Where in the world is their conscience? When they have trouble, they remember you. When things go smoothly, they forget."

The Brick Bed
土炕

她再不说话，两人就默默坐半天，吴三章起身走了。

又过了三个月，她病复犯，一睡倒再不得起来，她知道自己不行了。村里人轮流照看她，吴三章对她说：

"给秀秀母女打个电话吧，让她们接你去西安，住大医院看看，或许会好了呢。"

她不同意，说是活到时候了，不必告诉秀秀母女，更没必要进城去治了。果然第三天黎明，她气弱得只有出的，没有入的。村里人都围在土炕边，她说：

"都上炕坐吧，这土炕大，能坐得下。大家都来看我，我也死得下了。只是担心秀秀她们，害怕我这一死，她们如果再有个什么难了，可来找谁呀?!"

说罢，便咽了气，眼睛没有合住。

众人哭了一场，替她揉合了眼睛，把她埋在窑外的埝畔上。

窑空起来，村里没人去住，就锁了门。几年光景，没了

She had nothing to say. The two of them sat quietly for a while, then Wu Sanzhang rose to leave.

Three months later she had a relapse and could not rise from bed any longer. She knew she was not long for this world. Villagers took turns looking in on her, and Wu Sanzhang said to her: "Give Xiuxiu and her mother a call and have them send a car for you. You can try checking into a big hospital in Xi'an. Maybe you'll get better."

She did not agree and told him she had lived long enough. There was no need to tell Xiuxiu and her mother; there was still less need to get treatment in the city. Sure enough, at dawn on the third day, her vital force drained away and her breaths came haltingly. People of the village gathered around the brick bed. She said to them:

"Come up and sit on the bed—it will hold all of you. Since you're all here to see me, I can die with my mind at ease. I only worry about Xiuxiu and her mother: if they run into trouble again after I die, whom will they turn to?"

After speaking these words, she stopped breathing. Her eyes remained open.

All of them wept. They closed her eyelids, then buried her outside the cave, at the edge of an earthen berm.

The cave was now empty, but no villagers came to live in it, so a padlock was put on the door. The years took their toll,

烟火，窑在雨天里塌了，把大土炕埋在里边。后来，县上、省上的干部经常来下乡，好些女干部到羊儿沟，问起了她。知道人死了，窑塌了，都伤心落泪，怀恋那土炕，说土炕真好，又大，又舒服。

1981 年

and there was no cooking fire to keep dampness out. During a rainy spell the cave-house collapsed, burying the brick bed inside. Later, cadres from the county and province came on visits to the countryside. Quite a few female cadres who came to Yang'ergou asked about the woman. Hearing of her death and the cave's collapse, they shed tears of grief. They missed that brick bed. They said it was a fine bed, big and comfortable.

1981

The Brick Bed
土炕

秋　天①

　　九月三日，是天狗的生日。天狗属鼠，十二属相之首。

三十六岁的门槛年里，却仍是一种忌讳影子般摆脱不掉，干

什么事都提心吊胆。

---

　　① 节选自《天狗》。

Autumn[①]

Translated by Jun Liu

The third day of the ninth lunar month was Tiangou's birthday. He was born in the Year of the Rat, first of the Twelve Zodiac Animals. Tiangou was turning thirty-six and entering his inauspicious "Threshold Year," when taboos tail you like shadow and your heart is in your mouth with every action you take.

---

① An excerpt from *Tiangou*.

说起来，天狗在这事上够可怜的。王家的里亲外戚，人口不旺，正人也不多，爹娘下世后，大半就断绝了来往；小半的偶有走动，也下眼看天狗不是个能成的人物，情义上也淡得如水。他是舅家门上最大的外甥，舅死的时候，他哭得最伤心，可给舅写铭旌，做第一外甥的天狗，名字却排不上。已经死去的三姨的儿子在县银行当主任，有头有脸有妻有子，竟替换了天狗，天狗那时很生气，人没了本事，辈数也就低了？于是又跪倒在舅的坟前哭了一场。从此只和大姨感情笃。

大姨是天狗娘的姊妹里唯一幸存者，该老的人了，没老，她说是"牵挂天狗"的原因。牵挂天狗，最牵挂的是天狗的婚姻。眼看着天狗三十五岁上婚姻未动，就更恐慌三十六岁这门槛年，便反复叮咛这一年事事小心，时时上心。并一定要天狗在生日这天大过，以喜冲凶，消灾

Come to think of it, Tiangou is rather pitiful. The Wang family is a small one, and with few relatives on the paternal or the maternal side, and distinguished ones scarce too, there aren't many left to carry on the lineage. Since his parents passed away, most have ceased contact. The rest who occasionally visit look down on Tiangou, and reckon he'll never amount to anything. Naturally, familial ties have grown thin as water.

Tiangou is the eldest nephew of his mother's brother, and his was the most heart-broken wail heard when his uncle passed. But when it came to authoring the funeral banner, Tiangou, the First-born Nephew, wasn't even in the running for the honor. The son of his deceased third aunt is a director in the county bank, and this gent has it all: a wife and a son, and the all-important *face*, so it was his name on that banner, not Tiangou's. At the time, Tiangou was infuriated: *When a man hasn't proven himself capable, does his seniority by birth somehow drop a notch?* He knelt at his uncle's tomb and cried his heart out.

Ever since then, he has been emotionally close only to his eldest aunt, the last living sister of Tiangou's mother. Her time is overdue, but she's still hanging in there. "I'm just too worried for Tiangou's sake," as she puts it, and topping her worry list is her nephew's marriage. Seeing no hint of marital prospects while Tiangou was thirty-five, she's been panicking about his Threshold Year. "Be careful about each and every thing you do," she admonishes him at every chance, "don't let your guard down for one second." And she insisted that

秋天 Autumn

免祸。

给天狗过生日的，不是别人，却是师娘。她前三天就不让师徒二人去打井，九月初三里七碟子八碗摆了酒席。席间，大姨从江对岸过来。她先去天狗家里未找到天狗，来这里看着席面，倒说了许多感恩戴德的话。当时就将所带的挂面、面鱼放在柜上，又将一件衫子、一个红绸肚兜、一条红裤带交给天狗。这种以婴儿过岁的讲究对待三十六岁的天狗，天狗当场就笑得没死没活。大姨一走，他就要将这些东西让给五兴，师娘恼了脸，非叫他穿上不可。那神色是严肃的，天狗就遵命了。

现在，危险的一年即将完结，大姨又从江对岸过来，见天狗四肢强健，气血红润，念佛一般喜欢，说："看来你是个命壮的人，门槛年里没出大事，往后就更好了。"大姨说

Tiangou celebrate the critical thirty-sixth birthday with fanfare, so the happy event would overpower the bad luck, and vanquish potential disasters.

In the end, the one who hosted the celebrations was none other than Tiangou's Shiniang, his Master's wife. Three days ahead of the big day, she forbade her husband and his apprentice to do any well-digging. Come the third day of the ninth lunar month, she cooked up a lavish banquet.

During the feast, his eldest aunt came from the other side of the river. She had been to Tiangou's place and found no one. Taken aback at the table laden with dishes, she was quick to pronounce a string of blessings, place her handmade noodles and fish-shaped dough on the cabinet, and present Tiangou with a loose-fitting blouse, a red belt and a crimson silk *dudou* belly-wrap. Being pampered like a baby upon its first birthday, the thirty-six-year-old cackled until he was breathless. As soon as his aunt left, Tiangou tried to regift these lucky charms to Wuxing, his Shifu's son. But Shiniang pulled a long face and demanded that he don them then and there. She was dead serious, so Tiangou obeyed.

As Tiangou's year of peril draws to a close now, the old lady arrives again from across the river. Finding her nephew with four limbs intact, strong and sturdy, rosy and ruddy, she's as content as a devotee reciting the Buddhist sutras.

"Seems your destiny is a robust one. When nothing disastrous happens during your Threshold Year, the future is

秋天 Autumn

到快活处，就唠叨这王家总算没有灭绝，想起早死的姊妹，眼圈就红了。

"天狗，生日一过，就要动动你的婚姻了。阎王留姨在人世，姨不看着你成亲，姨就不得死去。你给姨说，这一年里，还没有物色着一个吗?"

天狗说："没有。"

姨说："姨给你瞅下一个，是个二婚，人倒体体面面，又带一个三岁娃娃，是春天离的婚，不知你可中意?"

天狗说："姨也糊涂了！我还见都没见过这人，怎么好说愿意不愿意?"

姨说："那你说说，你要啥样的女人?"

天狗支吾了半天，还是说不出口。大姨就拧了他的耳朵："这羞什么口。三十六七的人了，提说女人还脸红，心窍不开!"天狗在心里直笑大姨，天狗有什么不知道的！但听了大姨的话，却越发做出不好意思的样子，表明天狗是心

even brighter."

On that cheerful note, her prattle turns to the family lineage: Perhaps the Wang's won't come to an end after all. But then thoughts of her sisters, all of whom died ahead of their time, redden the rim of her eyes.

"Once your birthday is over, Tiangou, it'll be time to get things rolling with your marriage. The King of Hell has kept your auntie in this world, but unless she sees you tying the knot, she can't make her exit. Confide in your old auntie: Didn't you spot even one promising girl all last year?"

"Nope," admits Tiangou.

"Your auntie has got her eyes on one for you. She's a divorcée, but a very decent one. She has a three-year-old child, and she divorced just this spring. Might she please you?"

"Auntie, you must be going senile! I haven't even laid eyes on her. How do I know if I'd be willing?"

"Go on, spill the beans then. What sort of woman do you fancy?"

Tiangou hems and haws, but can't find the right words.

"What's there to be bashful about?" she chuckles, pinching his ear. "A man soon to turn thirty-seven who still blushes at the mention of a woman. Such a greenhorn!"

What could possibly be out there that Tiangou doesn't know about, he chortles under his breath at his doting auntie. Her words, however, leave him looking even more awkward. Tiangou is an innocent fellow, his aunt must know. But his

秋天 Autumn

实的人。不想弄巧成拙，大姨倒长吁短叹，再不问他。天狗

终于耐不住了，说："姨，有五兴娘好吗?"说完就屏住

了气。

大姨说："没五兴娘的性儿软，却比五兴娘要年轻呢。

天狗，你不懂女人，栽红薯要越大越好，讨女人是越小的越

金贵哩。"

天狗做出没听懂的样子。

大姨就扳过天狗的肩，发现肩背的衣服裂了一个口子，

拿针缝着，说："那寡妇有个娃，有娃也好，不是亲养的也

不见得对咱不孝。我对那寡妇提说了你，人家倒愿意，只是

说她娘家有个老娘和一个小兄弟，平日靠她养活。她要再

嫁，得给娘家出些钱。你现在手里攒了多少?"天狗说："有

三百。"大姨说："那是老虎嘴里的一个蝇子! 你还要好好攒

钱哩。"天狗心就凉了，说："既是这样，也就算了。"大姨

倚老卖老，说："算什么着? 这事你要不失主意! 你是不吃

effort backfires. She ceases her interrogation, sighing long and hard.

"Auntie," Tiangou can't resist asking, "is she as nice as, say, Wuxing's mother?" At that, he holds his breath.

"Not as gentle as Wuxing's mother, no, but she's much younger. You're naive about women, Tiangou. You aim to plant the biggest sweet potato, but when it comes to taking a wife, the younger, the more precious."

Tiangou still looks befuddled.

She pulls Tiangou over by the shoulder, spots a rip in his clothing and grabs a needle and thread. "That divorcée has a child," she says, beginning to stitch the tear, "which is not a bad thing. Her child isn't our own flesh and blood, but that doesn't mean that child won't look after us in our old age."

"I've mentioned you to her. She's not unwilling, but she said her elderly mother and a very young brother both rely on her support. If she is to remarry, some cash will need to go her family's way. So, how much savings do you have in hand?"

"Umm, three hundred or so," Tiangou replies. "A mere fly in a tiger's mouth!" exclaims she, "you need to save a bundle."

A chill stabs Tiangou in the heart. "If that's so, let's forget about it."

"Forget about what?" retorts auntie in that authoritative tone often voiced by seasoned folks. "Don't be naive! If you've never tasted candy, you don't know how sweet it can be. A

秋天 Autumn

糖不知糖甜，女人好处多哩，白日给你做饭，夜里给你暖脚，给你做伴说话，生儿育女，你敢再打马虎？几时我来领你去相看人家，把人先订下，钱你慢慢攒。"

三天后，天狗去见了那寡妇，人虽不是大姨说的光彩照人，却也整头平脸。回来将这事说给五兴娘，菩萨欢喜异常，说："这总算有了着落，天狗，你咬着牙，这几个月多出些力，手头把自己吃喝刻苦些，好生攒钱。"天狗说："那女的就是心太重，她不是为着找男人，倒是寻债主的。"女人说："哎，做妇道的，就是眼窝浅；可也难怪，啥事妇道人家都得前前后后地想得实在啊。"天狗说："师娘就不是这样！"师娘就笑了，骂一声"天狗贫嘴"。天狗是贫嘴，天狗不会文绉绉说甜蜜话，冷不丁就冒一句"酸话"，冒过了龇着白厉厉的牙笑。天狗又说："我跟她怎么总热火不起来？"女人瞧他说得认真，用白眼窝瞪着天狗："你嫌人家是寡

wife is nice in oh so many ways: cooking you meals in the day, warming your feet at night, someone to chat with and keep you company. Best of all, she'll bear you sons and daughters and raise them. How can you remain half-hearted about this? Some time soon I'll take you for a quick once-over, and fix the engagement. As for the bride-price, you can work on that at your own pace. "

Three days later, Tiangou pays the woman a visit. Not as radiant as portrayed by his aunt, but she's still well-proportioned. When he relates the trip to Wuxing's mother, she is thrilled.

"Well, looks like it's finally going be settled then, " says she. "Just grit your teeth and tighten your belt, Tiangou. Work harder the next few months and put aside every penny you can. "

"It's just that the woman seems so, so calculated: She's not looking for a husband, she's hunting for somebody she can milk for money. "

"Well, we womenfolk seldom see further than our nose, do we? But who can blame us, a woman has to weigh up everything and keep her feet on the ground. "

"Not so with my Shiniang!" protests Tiangou.

"Cheeky Tiangou!" she scolds him, chuckling.

Tiangou can be cheeky, that he admits. He's not one to fancify with sweet words, but he may blurt out something sour as a pickle, his teeth gleaming as he titters.

"How come I just don't hit it off with her?" he plows on,

妇?""这我倒不嫌弃。师娘，就是有比她再大的，只要人好，我还愿意哩!"话一出口，女人变了脸，天狗也觉得说漏了，两个人很是一阵别扭。女人就说她要去后山割黄麦菅晒柴，天狗也便起身走了。

临出门，女人叫住天狗，说:"天狗，夜里你擦黑就来，我给你擀长面吃。"

天狗说:"哟，日子真是过富裕了，晚上也吃长面?"

女人说:"不光长面，还有红鸡蛋呢! 你想想，明日是什么日子?"

天狗猛地记起明日是自己的生日，脸就红了，说:"师娘，我天狗没爹没娘，只有你记着我的生日，天狗不知怎么谢你呢!"

女人说:"瞧瞧，贫嘴又来了，天狗学会了不实在!"

天狗说:"我说的没一句不是心上来的。师娘，只要有

and his sober tone makes her look at him out of the corner of her eyes.

"So you turn your nose up at her because she's divorced?"

"No, I don't mind that. I'd be more than willing, Shiniang, even if it was someone older, as long as she's kind!"

This remark alters her countenance dramatically. That was more than a slip of tongue, Tiangou quickly realizes. The air sizzles momentarily with awkwardness. Then she announces she's off to the hillside behind the village to cut and dry tasselgrass for kindling. Tiangou gets up to leave too.

"Tiangou," she calls as he steps outside, "come back just before dark. I'll roll some longevity noodles for you."

"Life's really getting better, eh? longevity noodles for dinner?"

"Not just longevity noodles. Red-dyed eggs too! Take a wild guess: What day is tomorrow?"

It dawns on Tiangou—it's his very own birthday! "Shiniang," says he, cheeks flushing, "Tiangou has no father or mother. You're the only one who remembers my birthday. How can Tiangou thank you enough!"

"Tut, tut, there goes cheeky Tiangou again. He's learned to grease his tongue!"

"Every word I say comes from the bottom of my heart," pleads Tiangou. "Just a word from you, Shiniang, and Tiangou is

秋天 Autumn

你这一句话，天狗什么都够了。天狗能活九十九！至于过生日吗，我看算了，现在既然已经不是师傅的徒弟了，还要你操心？"

女人说："哟，媳妇八字还没一撇，就跟我说起外人话来了？怕也是我给你过的最后一个生日，等你成了家，明年我清清净净去你家吃那妹子擀的长面哩！今日无论如何要来，门槛年完了，也给你贺一贺！"

女人说着，眼里就媚媚地动人。没出息的天狗最爱见这眼光，也最害怕，他是一块冰做的，光一照就要化水儿了。

天狗回到家里，情绪很高。在屋檐下站着看了一阵嘶鸣的蝈蝈，就想着师娘的许多善良。想到热处，心里说，这女人必是菩萨托生，每个人来到世上都是有作用的，木匠的作用于木，石匠的作用于石；他师傅生来是作用于井，我天狗生来是作用于黄麦菅，而这女人则是为了美，为了善，恩泽这个社会而生的。天狗如此一番的见地，自己觉得很满意。

content. I can live to be ninety-nine! As for celebrating my birthday, let's just forget it. Since I'm no longer Shifu's apprentice, why should you bother?"

"What? Your marriage is still hanging in midair, and already you're talking to me like I'm an outsider? This could well be the last birthday dinner I'll rustle up for you. When you're properly wedded, I'll save myself the trouble next year and show up at your door to enjoy the longevity noodles hand-rolled by your woman! No matter what, you have to come tonight. Your Threshold Year is coming to an end, and that's well worth celebrating!"

As she speaks, her eyes sparkle with a charm at once desired and dreaded by soft-hearted Tiangou. If he were made of ice, a mere glance from those eyes would melt him.

Tiangou returns home in great spirits. Standing beneath the eave, he gazes at the long-horned grasshoppers chirping in their tiny cages, and muses about Shiniang's kindness. Warm and fuzzy, his thoughts glow:

Surely this woman is the reincarnation of a Bodhisattva? Each person enters the world to an end: A carpenter's purpose is to work wood and a mason's to shape rock; Shifu was born to bore wells, and Tiangou to put tasselgrass to good use; as for her, she must have come to this world purely to bequeath it with beauty and kindness...

Tiangou is quite satisfied with his epiphanies, but then a

秋 Autumn
天

忽然又想，菩萨现时要到山后去割草晒柴，那么细脚嫩手的人，能割倒多少柴火，我怎么不去帮她？就拿镰往后山走去。

后山上的草遍地皆是，将近深秋，草叶全黄了。黄麦菅一成熟，就变得僵硬，黄里又透了金的重色，风里沙沙沙作响。天狗站在草丛中，四面看着，却没见那女人出现，就弯腰砍割了一气，把三个草捆子扎起来立栽在那里了，他想等女人走来，出其不意地从草捆后冒出来，吓一吓她。

可是菩萨没有来。

天狗就拿了镰，走到一个洼子里的小泉边磨。水浅浅的，冲动着泉边的小草颤颤地抖，几只蚰蜒八脚分开划在水面，天狗的手已经接近了，它们还沉着稳健不动，但才要去捉，它们却影子一般倏忽而去。天狗用镰在水里砍了几砍，就倒在泉边的草窝里。看着一面干干净净的天，想着丹江对岸那个白脸子小寡妇，想着耷着奶子正在家擀长寿面的菩

new thought dawns: *The Bodhisattva, right now, is on her way to cut the coarse grass and dry it for fuel. Oh, those slender feet and tender hands, how much kindling can she reap? And why ain't I helping her right now?* Tiangou grabs his sickle and heads for the hillside.

The foot of the mountain is carpeted in grass. Towards the end of autumn, the blades have all turned champagne. Once it is ripe, the tasselgrass stiffens aureate with a heavy golden tinge, rustling in the wind. Tiangou stands amid the tussocks, craning his neck and looking about, but catches no glimpse of the woman. He bends down, slashing and hacking at a stretch, then binds the stalks into three bundles and stacks them together. When she arrives, he'll pop up from behind and give her a good fright.

But the Bodhisattva is nowhere in sight.

Tiangou carries his sickle down to a gully and hones it by a small spring. The puddle is shallow, and short blades of grass tremble in the ripples along its edges. A few centipedes glide on the water, rowing their multiple legs. Tiangou's hand is almost upon them, yet they remain perfectly composed; but just when he moves to snare one, the centipedes skim away like shadows.

He slashes the pool back and forth with the sickle, then slumps onto his back in the turf. Gazing into the speckless dome, he allows his thoughts to drift across the Scarlet River

秋 Autumn
天

萨，心里就又一阵美，像是坐了金銮殿充皇帝老儿。天狗这

些年里有了爱唱的德行，这阵心里便涌涌地想唱，便唱了：

想姐想得不耐烦呐，四两灯草也难担呐，

隔墙听见姐说话吧，我一连能翻九重山呐。

天狗唱完，兴致未尽，就又作想：这歌声谁能听到？于

是就想起另一位，拟着口气唱道：

郎在对门喊山歌，姐在房中织绫罗，

我把你发瘟死的早不死的唱得这样好哟，

唱得奴家脚跛腿软腿软脚跛，

踩不动云板听山歌。

to the fair-skinned young divorcée, then back to a house where the Bodhisattva is making hand-rolled noodles, breasts bulging. His heart swells with glee, as if he were the Emperor enthroned in the Imperial Palace.

Over the past few years Tiangou has nourished a penchant for song, and melodies are now surging in his chest. He sets them free:

> *Missing my lass puts me on edge,*
> *A bunch of lampwick grass too heavy for carrying.*
> *But hearing her voice from next door,*
> *Nine hills can I climb without tarrying.*

Each note lifts Tiangou's spirits higher than the last. *But who can hear my song?* Then the image of a certain someone surfaces, and he sings in her voice:

> *The lad yodels outside the gate,*
> *The lass weaving silk in her room.*
> *Why haven't you died of plague, O you sing so well!*
> *My legs are jelly, and my poor feet,*
> *Miss the Cloud Pedal, O your devilish songs!*

秋 Autumn
天

唱过了，天狗也累了，一边拿眼看山下的路，路上果然跑过来一个人，天狗认出那是师娘，偏不起身，只是拿歌子牵她过来，那女人也就发现了他，立着大喊："天狗，天狗!"

声音有些异样，天狗就站起来了。

女人也看见了天狗，就用哭腔喊叫："天狗，快来呀，你师傅出事啦!"

天狗立时停了歌声，也停了笑，拔脚跑下去，女人说："你怎么到山上来了。到处找不着你! 你师傅打井，井塌了，一块大石头把他压在下边，人都没办法救，你是打过井的，你快去救他啊，他毕竟做过你的师傅，天狗!"

天狗的血轰地上了头，扭身往堡子跑。女人却瘫在地上不能起来。天狗又过来架着她，飞一样到了刘家。刘家的院子里拥满了人，原来井打到二十五丈，出现一块巨石，师傅

At the end of the song, Tiangou is tired. He glances down the path below, and someone is running towards him. Shiniang, no doubt about it. But instead of standing up, he lays there and attempts to lure her over with his ditty. She spots him too, but stops abruptly.

"Tiangou! Tiangou!" she cries.

Something odd in her voice gets Tiangou up in a scramble.

"Come quick!" she blurts out, almost wailing, seeing his face. "Your Shifu has had an accident!"

Tiangou stops dead in mid-song, and his smile vanishes. He starts running down the hill toward her.

"What are you doing on the hillside? Couldn't find you anywhere!" she reproaches him. "Your Shifu was digging a well when it collapsed. He's stuck under a heavy rock and no one can pull him out. You've dug wells, Tiangou. Please, please come and save him. He was once your Master, after all!"

Whoosh! Tiangou hears the blood rushing into his brain. He wheels around and darts towards the village. But Shiniang has collapsed behind him. He strides back, drags her to her feet, and with an arm around her, flies towards the Liu's house.

The courtyard is jam-packed. The well-digging here had penetrated eighty-three meters when a boulder blocked the way. The master digger had chiseled a hole in the monolith,

用凿子凿了眼，装炸药炸了，二次返下井去，石头是裂了，却掏不出那一块大的，便从旁边挖土，土挖开了，只说那石头还是不动，就在下边用撬杠撬，不想石头塌下去，将他半个身子压住了。井上的人都慌了，下去又不敢撬石头，害怕石头错位伤了把式的性命，消息报给五兴娘，女人就四处找天狗。

天狗当即下井，师傅已经昏死过去了，石块还压在下身。他一边喊着"师傅"，一边刨师傅身下的土，又急，又累，又害怕稍不小心石头再压下来，好不容易把师傅拉出来，血淋淋地背在身上爬上井台。

几天几夜的抢救，井把式的命是保住了，保不住的却是他腰以下的神经。一个刚强的打井手艺人，从此瘫在了炕上，成了废人。

做农民的，什么都不怕缺，就怕缺钱；什么都应该有，

filled it with explosives and set it off. He went down the narrow shaft again and found the rock had cracked. But he couldn't extricate the largest chunk, so he dug at it from the side. When the soil was cleared away, thinking the rock wouldn't budge, he began leveraging it with a crowbar. All of a sudden, the rock gave way and pinned him down from the waist.

The crowd above panicked. They sent someone down but no one dared pry the rock further, one shift and it could cost the trapped man his life. When the news reached Wuxing's mother, she ran pell-mell, yelling for her husband's former apprentice.

Without a moment's hesitation, Tiangou negotiates the passage downward. Legs lodged under the rock, the Master is in a coma. "Shifu, Shifu—!" Tiangou calls, pawing frantically at the soil beneath the unconscious man. Desperate and exhausted, he fears that any moment the rock will press down further if he isn't careful. With a monumental effort he finally pulls Shifu free, hoists the bloodied survivor on his back, and clambers to the mouth of the well.

After several days and nights of intense care, the well-digger is clawed back from the verge of death. But the nerves below his waist are beyond repair. The iron-willed craftsman is henceforth wasted, doomed to lie paralyzed on the earthen *kang* bed.

A peasant can lack for anything except for money, and can

秋 Autumn
天

就是不敢有病。天狗的师傅英英武武打了几年井，如今打到这一步，这家人就完全垮了。女人在医院侍候了丈夫三个月，伤心落泪，眼睛肿烂，口舌生疮。天狗没有吃上那生日的长寿面，在后山上割倒的黄麦菅柴火也让谁家的孩子背走了。他再没有上山刨黄麦菅根，当然也再没有进省城。为了师傅的伤病，天狗和师娘背了把式住国营的医院，也找了民间的郎中。井把式还是站不起来。师傅的心也灰了，在炕上老牛似的哭，拿头往墙上撞。好说好劝，这要强心重的汉子才没有自尽，却日益伤心悲观，把脑子也搞坏了，显得痴痴呆呆的。

几个月的折腾，女人就失去了往常的光彩，形容憔悴，气力不支，蹲下干一阵起来，眼前就悠悠地浮一片黑云。更使她备受折磨的是家里的积蓄流水似的花去，日渐空虚，又

undergo anything, except for illness. For several years, Tiangou's Shifu bored wells like a true soldier, but when his career hit this low point, his household buckled like his legs.

For three months his wife waited at his bedside in the hospital, crying till her eyes were swollen and her mouth throbbed with blisters. Tiangou didn't have a chance to savor those longevity noodles for his birthday, and the kindling he bundled that afternoon was pilfered by some kids. He never returned to the hillside to dig up tasselgrass roots for whisk bristles, nor did he visit the provincial capital again to hawk them.

To seek a cure for Shifu, Tiangou carried him on his back to state-run hospitals accompanied by Shiniang, and together they sought out famed country healers far and wide. Still, the well-digger cannot stand on his own two legs. In the end he is resigned, moaning like an aged ox on the bed and banging his head against the wall. A relentless flow of encouragement is kept up to talk the proud and ambitious man out of suicide. But his free fall into despondency seems to have damaged his brain, and most of the time he just appears absent.

These few grueling months cost the woman her former luster, leaving her haggard and frail. When she stands up after sitting on her heels doing chores, a dark mist envelops her vision. But even more torturous is watching the family savings trickling away like water. Despite their economic means being depleted day by day, she mustn't even raise her voice in front

秋 Autumn
天

不敢对丈夫半句高声，常在没人处哭。

天狗看着，心里如刀扎，想自己不能代替了师傅。师傅是有长久手艺的人，能代替他瘫在炕上，这个家就不会这般受罪；看着师娘如此可怜，比天狗自己瘫在炕上还要难受。可天狗不是这家的人，只能在炕头劝说师傅，在院里安慰女人。帮着种地、喂猪、出圈粪；出外请医生抓药，就拿自己的钱来支应。

一场事故，把人囫囵地改变了性格。井把式褪了专横，女人变得刚强，天狗说过，"有了女人就长大了"，现没个伴他的女人，天狗也长大了。

这天，天狗又割了几斤肉和豆腐提来，女人说："天狗，你要总是这样，我也就恼了！这家里成了无底的黑窟窿，你有多少积存能填得满?!"天狗说："师娘，现在就不要说这

of her husband; all she can do is sob in a deserted corner.

Observing all this, Tiangou feels his own heart being pierced by a dagger. *If only I could swap places with Shifu! He possesses a lifelong talent, if only I could lie paralyzed on the* kang *in his stead, this family would be spared such torture!* Moreover, the sight of Shiniang in such a pitiful state makes Tiangou more distressed than if it were him lying there motionless.

But Tiangou is not a member of this family, and his place is by the head of the *kang* counseling Shifu, or in the courtyard comforting Shiniang. Aside from helping her tend the fields, feed the swine and clean the pigsty, he goes out looking for doctors and pays for the herbal concoctions out of his own pocket.

It takes an accident to completely transform a person. While the well-digger shed his despotic skin, his wife has grown tough. "When a man gets a woman, he matures," Tiangou used to proclaim. Yet with no companion at his side, Tiangou has somehow put on another ten years.

One day, Tiangou shows up again with a kilo of meat and a chunk of tofu in his hands.

"Tiangou," frowns Shiniang, "I'll get angry if you keep this up! This household has turned into a bottomless black hole. Your savings will never fill it!"

"Don't you worry about it now, Shiniang," replies

秋天 Autumn

些话，我一个人毕竟好将就。"

女人说："你也不是有金山银山，这么长时间也没去做刷子卖，你是另有什么手艺不成？你把钱花光了，那江对岸的女的怎么娶得回来？"

天狗没有给师娘说明。前天夜里，大姨又过江来找了他，说是那小寡妇有了话，问这边钱筹得怎样，若月底还是拿不出一千元，她就不再等了，有钱的几个光棍都在托媒了。天狗生了气，说："看谁钱多让她给谁去；我有一千元，一千元我天狗可以买十头猪给师傅补身子哩！"话说得难听，大姨好生骂了一顿，问他想不想要个儿子？天狗说得更粗野："我一千元放在那里，生的也是钱儿子！"大姨气得脸色煞白，吵了一夜，不欢而散。

师娘当然不知道这件事，还是说："天狗，眼看就是三月三乡会了，女婿都走丈人，你虽说没结婚，却也该到对岸

Tiangou, "I'll get by one way or the other by myself."

"You're not sitting on a mountain of gold," she replies, "for some time now you haven't made a single brush to sell. Do you have some other skills up your sleeve? If you empty your pockets, what will be left to wed that woman across the river?"

Tiangou hasn't been up front with Shiniang. The night before last, his aunt crossed the river bearing a message from the young woman. How was it going with the money, she wanted to know. "If you can't come up with one thousand *yuan* by month's end, then I'm done waiting. Quite a few moneyed bachelors have sent their matchmakers."

"Let that greedy woman sell herself to the highest bidder!" spat Tiangou. "A thousand bucks in my coffer? I could get ten plump porkers with that kind of money to bolster Shifu's health!"

This blunt comment earned him a fine dressing down. "Well, lad, do you still want a son or not?" rebuked his aunt.

"If I just put that sum aside, it'll at least lay me some copper sons!" barked Tiangou boorishly.

The old woman trembled ashen. The quarrel lasted the best part of the night before she stormed off.

"Tiangou," continues Shiniang, ignorant of his squabble with his aunt, "the Country Fair is just around the corner on the third day of the third lunar month. All the young men are

秋 Autumn
天

那家去。这肉既然买回来，咱就不要吃，我夜里再蒸二十个馍，你明日提前去走走吧。"

天狗听了，一时心火上攻，竟忘记了自己是在这苦难的菩萨面前，焦躁地说："我不去!"

女人说："你敢胡说!"

瘫了的师傅在上屋土炕上全听见了，就敲着炕沿叫天狗，天狗进去，师傅说："你怎能不去? 你想老死了做绝鬼?!"说罢拉天狗坐下，缓了口气又说："师傅现在是没用的人，别的话你可以不听，只要你听一句，明日乖乖去江对岸，这身上衣服也成油匠穿的了，夜里让你师娘洗一把，唵!"

天狗这才说了实话："人家早不成啦!"

说完也不再解释，走出门，一直从院子里走出去了。

井把式和女人倒一时愣了，末了女人就哭出声来。

calling on their fathers-in-law. You'd better cross the river to visit her too, even though you aren't hitched yet."

"Anyhow, since you've bought the meat, let's not waste it. I'll also steam some buns tonight, so you can bring something to visit her tomorrow, ahead of the Country Fair."

The kind offer sets a wild bush fire in his heart. "I'm not going!" snaps Tiangou, completely forgetting that the Bodhisattva in front of him is trapped in suffering herself.

"How dare you!" she chides him.

Lying in the main room, the Master overhears everything and calls for Tiangou, banging the rim of his earthen *kang* bed. "How can you not go?" he asks as soon as Tiangou sets his foot inside. "You want to die alone and be a ghost remembered by no offspring?"

He pulls Tiangou by the hand to sit by his side. "Your Shifu is a useless lump now," he says, drawing a few breaths. "Ignore whatever I say as you like, but not this. Cross the river tomorrow, and make no fuss about it. Look at you, that coat is worse-worn than a painter's. Let your Shiniang give it a good scrubbing tonight. Now go—!"

"But, but that woman brushed me off long ago!" admits Tiangou finally.

Not bothering with an explanation, he exits the room, strides straight across the courtyard and out the front gate.

For a brief moment, the well-digger and his wife are both dumbstruck. Then she begins to sob.

秋天 Autumn

夜里师娘来到天狗的家里，问清了原委，知道一切因自家的拖累所致，就连连叫"造孽"！骂天狗不该为她家花了积存，又骂小寡妇认钱不认人，下贱坏子。天狗见女人骂自己，越发觉得这女人贤惠可敬。女人骂着骂着，就骂了自己，哭泣不止。

天狗立在那里倒真像个手足无措的孩子。

女人说："天狗，是我家害了你，这我和五兴爹一辈子有赎不完的罪。事情落到这田地，我家里是空了，你也空了，即使你天狗还有分文，我也不让你再往我家里贴赔。可这个家，有出的没入的，啥事都要钱，我思谋了，还是让五兴回来干干别的事吧！"

天狗说："师娘，这使不得。五兴先头耽误了几天学习，好不容易让他又复了学，就是再穷再苦，也不敢误了五兴的

At night she goes to Tiangou's place and learns all the details. "What a sin!" she exclaims when it's clear that her family's misfortune is the undoing of Tiangou's courtship. She reprimands Tiangou for squandering his life's savings on her household.

"That low-lying bitch!" she curses, "all her eyes are on the money and she doesn't give a hoot who she's marrying!"

Though his name pops up every so often in her strong language, Tiangou only finds Shiniang more virtuous and respectable. On and on she cusses, then she turns her ire on herself and can't stop weeping. Tiangou, meanwhile, stands there rooted like a child, at a loss where to put his hands or feet.

"Tiangou," she says between sobs, "we are the only ones to blame for this. It's a sin Wuxing's Father and I cannot atone for in this life. Now that things have come to this wretched end—our family is stone broke, and you stand no better off— even if you manage to put aside a few pennies, Tiangou, I won't allow you to waste it on us!"

"Just look at our household: Money floods out but never seeps in, and we are cash-strapped in every corner. I've been thinking lately, maybe it's better to bring Wuxing back home and let him try his hand at something else!"

"Shiniang," pleads Tiangou, "please don't. Wuxing missed several days of school last time, and it wasn't easy to get him back in class again. No matter how dire things get, his

秋天 Autumn

学业。"

女人怎不明晓这层道理。可妇道人家是一副软心肠，经天狗一番道理之后，同意了不让五兴停学。可回到家里，一进屋，眼看着狼狈不堪的丈夫，一颗心又转了。这对中年夫妇一夜没有睡好，一会决定让五兴停学，说停学好；一会又不让停学，说不停学好。拉屎撒尿做不了主，井把式就大声吸着鼻子，哭了，"这都是我害了你们娘儿，害了人家天狗，我怎么就不死呢！你给我买包老鼠药来，让我喝了，反正活着没用，也不花钱吃药了！"女人听了这话，两股眼泪流下，说道："他爹，你别说这话，家里人嫌弃你了吗？你就是睡在这里任事不干，你也是这一家的定心骨。你要再说这话就是拿刀子杀我。你是还嫌我心没伤透吗？"男人就再不作声。

夫妇俩自结婚以来说了这最多的一场话，才各自深深体会到对方的温暖；生活的苦绳拴住了一对蹦跶的蚂蚱，他们

studies must not be disrupted. "

About this, she understands only too well. Being a soft-hearted woman, she allows herself to be persuaded not to pull her son out of school. But the moment she catches sight of her husband's abject form, her heart turns the other way.

It's a turbulent night for the middle-aged couple. One moment they decide to end Wuxing's studies, agreeing that's the best option; the next moment they oppose the idea. Unable to relieve himself or wipe his own bottom, the well-digger breaks out in frustrated tears.

"I've dragged you and Wuxing down along with Tiangou, " he says in between loud sniffling. "Damn it, why can't I just kick the bucket! Go get me a packet of rat poison and let me swallow it. At least I can save you some money on remedies! "

"Stop it, Wuxing's Father! " she begs, tears streaming down her cheeks. "Does anyone here ever look down on you? You're the backbone of this household, even if all you do is lie there and sleep. When you speak like that, you're just plunging a dagger in my heart. Do you think it's not already in pieces, my heart? "

Her man falls silent. Never before has the couple confided so much in each other, and their heart-to-heart helps them appreciate the other's warmth. The bitter twine of life has entangled the struggling pair of grasshoppers by the legs. Neither can bear to abandon the other.

秋 Autumn
天

谁也离不得谁。夜深了，油灯在界墙的灯窝里叭叭地响过一阵，油尽灯灭，女人重要点灯，男人说："算了。"为了省下一根火柴和一盏油，黑夜里泪眼在闪着光，男人被平放着睡下了，失去了知觉的双腿日渐萎缩，女人在被窝里为他揉搓，活动血脉，在扳着下身为男人翻了几次身后，女人就脱得光光的猫儿似的偎在丈夫的身边睡着了。睡到四更，女人突然被男人摇醒，她叫道："你咋没瞌睡？"男人说："我睡不着，我有一件事想给你说哩。"女人就坐起来，拥着被子，被子的一角湿漉漉的，是男人流下的眼泪。月光从窗棂里昏昏地照进来，女人看着丈夫一张被痛苦扭歪的脸。

男人说："我好强了一辈子，也自私了一辈子。和你做夫妻了十几年，我没有好好待你，这是我现在一想起来就心愧的事。我现在是完了，到死也离不了这面土炕了。人常说'病人心事多'，我是终日在想，啥事都想过了，想过死。你

The night grows old. The flame in the oil lamp crackles briefly in the niche on the wall, and then the oil is drained and the light fizzles out. She readies to light it again. "Leave it," says her husband. To save a match and a tad of lamp fuel, she lays him flat on his back, and two pairs of eyes glisten with tears in the dark night. Day by day his numb legs are shriveling, his wife massages them under the quilt to stimulate circulation. Grappling with his legs, she turns him over a few times, then strips naked and snuggles up by her man like a kitten before falling asleep.

In the small hours of the night, she wakes up in a shudder and finds her husband gently nudging her. "Trouble sleeping?" she murmurs.

"Didn't catch a wink. I've got something to tell you."

She sits up, gathers the quilt over her shoulders and touches a wet corner. It is soaked in his tears. Through the latticed window comes dim moonlight, barely enough for her to see his grief-torn visage.

"All my life I've been fighting to take first place," he begins, "and I was damn full of myself. For nearly two decades we've been man and wife, but I never treated you properly. Just the thought of it fills my heart with remorse."

"I'm done for. I won't get out of this bed until my dying day. 'The sick over-think,' they always say, and I've been lying here thinking, day and night, about everything, my final

骂了我，你骂是对的，我也没脸面再去死，我就活着吧。可咱家里，总不能这样下去啊，五兴他娘！因此上我就思想，你可以不离开我，我还是你的男人，但世上都是男人养活女人，女人怎能养活了男人，那南北二山都有'招夫养夫'的……"

女人静静地听男人叙说，越听越有些害怕，听到最后，一把将井把式的口捂住了，说："我不听，我不听，你睡在炕上胡想了些什么呀！"眼泪吧嗒地掉在被面上。

招夫养夫，深山里是有这种习俗的。平日里菩萨女人也听说过这种事例，只当是一种新闻，一种趣谈。现在丈夫竟要她充当这事例中的角色，她浑身痉挛，抖得像筛糠。

男人见女人如此悲凄，自己也裂心断肠，长吁短叹，说："我这样说，是我这男人的羞耻。可你不让我死，又不

moment in particular. You told me off and you were right to do so. I'm too ashamed to die; I reckon I'll just hang on. But this household of ours, we can't let it continue like this forever, Wuxing's Mother!"

"And so I've been thinking, you know, you don't have to leave me, and I, I'll still be your man. But it's always been the man who provides for his woman in this world. How can a man live off his wife?

"In the North and South Mountains, you see, there are those who 'marry anew to support the old'…"

She remains perfectly still, a clutch of fear gripping her throat more tightly with each word he utters. In the end, she reaches out and covers his mouth.

"Stop," she says in a quavering voice. "I'm not listening to this. What horrible thoughts have wormed into your head while you lie here!" Dollops of tears drop onto the already damp quilt.

Getting married again in order to support an existing husband—such customs do still linger deep in the mountains. This Bodhisattva of a woman has heard tell of such things, but that was nothing more than gossip, something to spice up the conversation. Now, her very own husband is begging her to play a role in such a drama! She shakes from head to toe like grain being winnowed to separate it from the chaff.

Her misery makes her husband feel his own heart and guts

这样，你是让我睡在这里看你受苦受难，我不死在绳上药上，也会用心杀了我自己！"

女人就扑在男人身上，泣不成声："只要为了你，我什么都可以做得，可你让我招夫，我到哪儿去招？哪个单身男子肯进咱的门？就是有人来，好了还罢，若是个坏的，待你不好，那我哭都没眼泪了！"

夫妇俩抱头哭到天明。天明的时辰，听见远远的后山上有狼的噪声，犹如人在呼号。

清早，女人又要去后山割草晒柴，男人叮咛说到阳坡割，不要去阴洼，若遇见什么狗了，先"狼，狼！"叫喊试探，以防中了狼的伪装；若不慎惊撞了马蜂，万不要跑，用草遮了头脸就地装死。女人一一记在心上，走了。男人见女人一走，就在家大放了悲声，惊动了街坊。有人进来，他就

are being wrenched and shredded. "As a man it's shameful for me to bring it up," he concedes, sighing deeply. "But you won't let me die or follow my suggestion, you are condemning me to lie here watching you suffer, yet unable to lift a finger. Even if I don't die by rope or poison, my aching heart alone will snuff me out twice over!"

"I'd do anything if it's for you," she wails, throwing herself onto his heaving chest. "But it's a new husband you are asking me to find! Where shall I even begin? What single man in his right mind would set foot in our door? And even if someone does come, it might be bearable if he's decent; if he treats you like dirt, I'd cry my eyes dry!"

Locked in one another's arms, the couple cries until daybreak. At dawn, wolf howls come from the mountains far behind the village, as if someone were moaning in agony.

Early in the morning, she heads again for the hillside behind the village to cut grass and dry it for kindling. "Go to the sunny slope," advises her husband, "never go down to the shady dell. If you spot something that looks like a dog, first cry 'Wolf! WOLF!' Don't fall for that beast playing a dog. And if it happens that you startle some wasps, never ever run. Just cover your hair and face in grass, and play dead on the spot..."

His wife repeats twice to herself everything he said, and sets out. As soon as her footsteps fade, the well-digger breaks

秋天 Autumn

115

求人去把天狗找来，说他有话要叙说。

天狗苦苦闷闷窝在家里，什么事也慌得捏不到手里，就无聊地编织起蝈蝈笼子来。三月的蝈蝈还没活跃，没有清音排泄他的烦愁，就痴痴看着空笼出神。他到了师傅的炕边，以为师傅又要说让五兴退学的事，便说："师傅，有我天狗在，我天狗就永远是你的徒弟，我不是那喂不熟的狗，我天狗是没大本事的，可我不会使师傅这一家败下去，无论如何，五兴要让他好好念书。"

师傅说："天狗，也怪我先前瞎了眼窝，没让你跟我继续打井。人就是这没出息的，只有出了事，才会明白，可明白了又什么也来不及了。你给师傅说，江对岸那小寡妇真的吹了？"

天狗说："吹了，那号女人只盯着钱！甭说她不愿意了，

into a heart-wrenching howl. In no time flat, an alarmed neighbor races in.

"Please," urges the invalid, "please bring me Tiangou. I've something really important to tell him."

Meanwhile, Tiangou has been cooped up at his home, sulking. Whatever he picks up refuses to take shape in his fingers, and out of boredom he succumbs to braiding a grasshopper cage. It's just the third month after the Spring Festival, and long-horned grasshoppers aren't active yet. With no chirping to relieve his troubled thoughts, Tiangou gazes vacantly at the empty cage.

By the time he reaches Shifu's side, Tiangou is prepared lest the topic of Wuxing abandoning school come up. "Shifu," says he reassuringly, "as long as Tiangou remains standing, I am forever your disciple. I am a 'Celestial Dog,' true to my name, not a mongrel that bites the hand that feeds it. True, this 'Celestial Dog' may not amount to much, but Tiangou will fight tooth and nail to keep Shifu's family above water. We must not distract Wuxing from his books, no matter what."

"I must have been blind as a bat, Tiangou, to kick you out of the well," says his former Master. "Good for nothing, every man is. Only when disasters befall him does he come to his senses, but by then it is too late. Now, be honest with your Shifu: That woman across the river, is she really a lost cause?"

"She's history," admits Tiangou, "that sort of woman is born with itchy palms! Put aside the fact that she's unwilling

秋 Autumn
天

就是她那德行，十七、十八的开的是一朵花，我走过去拾一

片瓦盖了理也不理。你想想，要是师娘也是那样的人，她不

知早离开你多长日子了。"

师傅说："唉，你师娘是软性子，受了我半辈子气，可

她心善啊，逢着这样的老婆，我李正什么也就满足了。可如

今，她受的苦太重，毕竟是一个妇道人家，地里没劳力，里

外没帮手，不让五兴退学吧，要吃要喝又要花钱，还加上伺

候我这废人，一想到这，我心就碎了。天狗，我想让她走一

条招夫养夫的路，你实话对我说，使得使不得？"

天狗听了，心里不禁一阵疼。伤残使师傅变成了另一个

人。做出这般决定，师傅的心里不知流过了多少血？不行，

不行，天狗摇着头。可不走这条路，可怜的师娘就跳不出苦

海，天狗头又摇起来。天狗没有回天力，只是拿不定主意地

to marry the likes of me, given her behavior, if she were a maiden of just over seventeen and blooming like a dainty flower, I'd just stomp right over, pick up a tile, dump it on her head, then go on my way and never once look over my shoulder. Just think about it, if Shiniang were even remotely like that wench, she'd have walked out on you ages ago."

"Indeed," sighs the Master, "your Shiniang is such a dove, putting up with my quick temper ever since we married. A golden heart, that woman surely has. Having chanced upon a wife like this, I, Li Zheng, ought to be content with whatever life throws my way."

"But she's suffering too much these days. She's just a frail woman, after all, and there's no labor in the fields, or any helping hand inside the home or out. If we don't take Wuxing out of school, who's there to help prepare the food and drink and foot the bill for everything else, and wipe the arse of an invalid on top of that? The very thought makes my heart shatter.

"I've been thinking, Tiangou, there is a path she can take: 'Marry anew to support the old.' Tell me from the bottom of your heart, would that work?"

Tiangou's heart throbs with pain. *His crippled state has transformed Shifu into someone else. To reach this decision, how his heart must have bled!* No, no, Tiangou tells himself, shaking his head. *But, if she doesn't take this path, my poor Shiniang may never escape the Sea of Suffering.* Again his head begins to shake. The lack of power to undo what Heaven

摇头。两人沉默了半天，天狗说："师傅，这事你给师娘

说过?"

师傅说："说不通。可从实际来看，这样好。这又不犯

法，别人也说不上笑话。你说呢?"

天狗说："那有合适的人吗?"

做师傅的却不作回答，为难了许久，拉天狗坐近了，

说："作难啊，天狗，谁能到这里来呢? 你师娘一听我说这

话，就只是哭。我想，你师娘那心肠你也是知道的，这堡子

里也没几个能赶上她的。虽说是快四十的人了，但长相上还

看不出来……"说着就直直地看天狗的脸。

天狗并不笨，品得出师傅话里的话，心里别地一跳，将

头低下了。

屋子里沉沉静静。

has ordained leaves Tiangou indecisive. For a long while, neither speaks.

"Shifu," says he in the end, "have you talked this over with Shiniang?"

"She won't listen to reason," says he, "but mine is the best option, if we're being honest with ourselves. We wouldn't be breaking any laws, or turn ourselves into a laughing stock. What do you say?"

"Then," asks Tiangou tentatively, "do you have someone in mind?"

No reply comes. His Master is visibly struggling. In the end he pulls his ex-apprentice over. "It's next to impossible, Tiangou," he begins, "who'd come to our place? If I so much as mention one word of it, your Shiniang dissolves in tears."

"What I have in mind is, by now you must know your Shiniang by heart and soul, there are less than a handful in this whole village who can claim themselves her equal. She's going on forty, there's no denying it, but you can't tell from her looks..." His voice trails off, but his eyes are glued to Tiangou's.

Tiangou, no fool, has heard what his Master didn't say. His heart skips a beat, and he suddenly becomes interested in his feet.

Once again, silence floods the room. Tiangou slips down the *kang* and slumps onto the circular straw mat.

秋天 Autumn

天狗从炕上溜下来，坐在了草蒲团上。院子里，女人背着高高的一背篓柴火进来，在那里咚地放了。院墙的东南角上，积攒的柴草已俨然成山。女人一头一脸的汗，头发湿得贴在额上，才要坐下歇口气，瞧见天狗从堂屋走出来，就叫了一声"天狗!"

天狗痴痴地从院子里走出去，头都没有转一下。

三天里，丹江岸上的堡子，沉浸在三月三乡会的节日里。农民们在这几天停止一切劳作，或于家享乐，或频繁地串亲戚。未成亲的女婿们皆衣着新鲜，提四色大礼去拜泰山泰水。泰山泰水则第一次表现出他们的大方，允许女儿同这小男人到山上去采蕨菜。三月里好雨水，蕨菜嫩得弹水。采蕨人在崖背洼，在红眼猫灌丛，也采着了熟得流水的爱果。天狗家的后窗正对着山，窗里装了一幅画，就轻轻唱出了往

Outside, a huge pile of branches enters the courtyard. Shiniang is bent double under a basket on her back piled high with branches. "*Thud*!" she unloads her burden at the southeastern corner of the wall, where firewood and grass for kindling are stacked haphazardly into a sizeable hill. Strands of soaked hair stuck on her forehead, she is just sitting down to catch her breath when Tiangou emerges.

"Tiangou!" she calls.

Eyes glazed, Tiangou marches straight out the gate without glancing back.

Commencing on the third day of the third lunar month, for three days the fortified village perched on the bank of the Scarlet River is immersed in the Country Fair's festivities. Peasants cease their labor, enjoying themselves at home or calling on their relatives and friends nonstop.

Brightly dressed up for the occasion, the betrothed men visit their future parents-in-law—"Mount Tai" and "River Tai"—with four types of fine offerings. Mount Tai and River Tai also take this occasion to show their generosity for the first time by permitting their daughter to join her young fiancé in gathering wild fern in the mountains. The rich rain that comes with the third lunar month has nurtured the bracken fern so well that sap drips off the tender shoots upon the lightest touch. In a glen behind a cliff, amidst a thicket of Red-Eyed Cat, the fern-gatherers also harvest the fruit of love, juicy and ripe.

秋天 Autumn

年三月三里要唱的歌：

远望乖姐矮陀陀噢，

背上背个扁挎箩哟，

一来上山去采蕨噢，

二来上山找情哥哟，

找见情哥有话说。

唱完了，天狗就叹一口气，把窗子关上，倒在炕上蒙被子睡了。天狗从来没有这样恍惚过，他不愿意见到任何人，直到夜里人都睡下了，天狗就走到堡子门洞上的长条石上。旧地重至，触景生情，远处是丹江白花花的沙滩，滩上悄然无声。今晚的月亮再也不是天狗要吞食的月亮，但人间的天狗，三十七岁的童男，心里却是万般感想。师傅的女人，师

The back window of Tiangou's house opens to the mountains. Admiring the framed landscape tableau, he quietly intones the lyrics he used to sing for this rural festival:

Chubby'n'short there goes my darling,
on her back an oblong basket.
For fern in the hill she is coming,
with a sharp eye out for her beau,
O so much has she her love to tell!

At the end of the song, Tiangou sighs deeply. Then he pulls the window shut, throws himself onto the *kang*, covers his head with the quilt and tries to get some shuteye. Never before has he been so listless. He doesn't wish to encounter anyone, so it is after all are sound asleep that he finally emerges.

Soon he finds himself at the wall enclosing the village and sits on the stone slab at the entry into the passageway. This is the second time he has come down here deep at night, and the familiar scenery triggers a jumbled mix of feelings. In the distance, the Scarlet River's shoal shimmers white, not a sound hails from that direction. There is no eclipse tonight, and the moon is not the one to be devoured by the fabled Celestial Dog. But here on earth, the mythical canine's namesake, already thirty-seven and still a virgin, is besieged by troubled thoughts.

娘，菩萨，月亮，使天狗认识到了一个实实在在的女人。在一年多徒弟生涯里，在十几年一个堡子的邻里生活中，天狗喜欢这女人。女人的一个腰身，一步走势，一个媚眼，都使他触电一样地全身发酥，成百上千次地回忆着而生怕消失。他天狗曾怀疑过和害怕过自己的这种感情，警告过自己不应该有这种非分之想。但天狗惊奇的是，对于这个女人，他只是充满着爱，而爱的每次冲动却绝对地逼退了别的任何邪思歪念。天狗不是圣人，他在这女人面前能羞耻，能检点，也算得是圣人了。所以，天狗也敢将这种喜欢和爱，作为自己的生命所需，变成一副受宠的样子，在这菩萨面前要做出孩子般的腼腆和柔顺。

月食的夜里，女人在这里为丈夫和另一个小男人祈祷而唱乞月的歌，天狗也为女人唱了两首歌。歌声如果有精灵，是在江水里，还是在草丛里？

Via Shiniang—at once his Master's wife, Tiangou's Moon and a Bodhisattva—Tiangou has come to understand the meaning of a real woman. Throughout the year he served as Shifu's apprentice, and in the dozen years he has lived as Shiniang's neighbor in the same village, Tiangou has long nursed a soft spot for this woman. A twist of her waist, her gait, or a glance from those eyes that speak never fail to electrify his body. And he savors those charged moments for hundreds, no, thousands of times, lest they fade into oblivion.

Tiangou has doubted and even dreaded these feelings. *You should never harbor such improper thoughts,* he admonishes himself time and again. But surprising even himself, he finds only pure love in his heart for this woman, and each loving impulse has kept any racy whim at bay. Tiangou is certainly no sage, but if he does feel shame before this woman, and is able to rein himself in, surely that would rank him among the virtuous? And so Tiangou emboldens himself to regard this affection, even love, as a need essential to his very life, and he assumes the demeanor of a child, shy and obedient before his Bodhisattva, basking in her favor.

On that night of lunar eclipse, it was right here that she sang a song to bring back the moon and prayed for the safety of her husband, and a younger man too. That night, Tiangou also sang two ballads just for her. *If songs had souls, would they inhabit the river,* he wonders, *or the grass?*

秋天 Autumn

"现在要我做她的第二个男人吗?"

说出这话的,不是他天狗,也不是他天狗爱着的师娘,竟是自己的师傅,女人的真正的丈夫!天狗该怎么回答呢?"我愿意,我早就愿意!"天狗应该这么说,却又说不出口。她是师娘,是天狗敬慕和依赖的母亲般的人物,天狗能说出"我是她的男人"的话吗?天狗呀,天狗,你的聪明不够用了,勇敢不够用了,脸红得像裹了红布,不敢看师傅,不敢看师娘,也不敢看自己。面对着屋里的镜,面对着井底的水,面对着今夜头顶上明明亮亮的月亮,不敢看,怕看出天狗是大妖怪。

第四天,是星期天。五兴从学校回来,到江边的沙地上挖甘草根。

天狗看见了,问:"五兴,你掘那甘草做甚?"

五兴说:"给我娘采药。"

天狗慌了:"采药?你娘病了?什么病?"

五兴说:"我从学校回来,娘和多吵架,娘就睡倒了,

And now, should I become her second husband?

The one who brought this up was not Tiangou, nor his beloved Shiniang, but his very own Shifu, her true lawful husband! And how should he reply? "I'm willing, and I've always wanted to!" That's what Tiangou ought to say, but he just cannot bring himself to utter those words. She is Shiniang—a motherly figure Tiangou venerates and depends upon—and who is he to boldly proclaim, "I am her man!"?

Tiangou, Tiangou, where have your wits and bravery gone? His face scarlet as if covered in red cloth, he dares not steal a glance at Shifu, Shiniang, or even himself. Whether he's facing the mirror in the house, the water deep in the well, or the moon that shines exceptionally bright tonight, no, he dares not look—*might Tiangou be that colossal monster, after all?*

The fourth day is Sunday. Wuxing, freshly back from school, goes to the sandy banks along the river to scavenge liquorice root.

"Wuxing," greets Tiangou when he spots the boy, "what are you digging for?"

"Herbal medicine for my Mum," replies the boy.

"Oh?" panics Tiangou, "is your mother ill?"

"I came back from school," relates Wuxing, "and my parents had an argument. Mum took to bed and said her

说是肚子鼓，心疼。爹让我来采的。"

天狗站在沙地上一阵头晕。

"天狗叔，你怎么啦？"

"太阳烤得有些热。五兴，念书可有了长进？"

"天狗叔，我娘又不让我念了。"

"不是已给她说好不停学了吗？"

"我娘说的，她跪着给我说的，说家里困难，不能老拖累你，要我回来干活。"

天狗默默回到家里，放声大哭了。他收拾了行李，决意到省城去，从这堡子悄悄离开，就像一朵不下雨的云，一片水，走到天外边去。但是天狗走不动。天狗在堡子门洞下的三百七十二台石级上，下去三百台，复上二百台。这时的天狗，若在动物园里，是一头焦躁的笼中狮子；若在电影里，是一位决战前夜地图前的将军。

天狗终于走到了师傅家的门口。

tummy's swollen and her heart aches. So Dad sent me down here."

A dizzy spell sweeps over Tiangou as he stands uncertainly on the sandy shoal.

"Uncle Tiangou, are you alright?"

"Umm, the sun's a bit hot today. How about your studies, Wuxing, making good progress?"

"Mum told me not to go anymore, Uncle Tiangou."

"Didn't we persuade her not to stop your studies?"

"But it's Mum who said it, and she said it down on her knees: 'Things are tough for the family these days, we mustn't burden your Uncle Tiangou like this.' And she told me to come home to work."

Tiangou bites his tongue and returns home, where he bursts out crying. He packs his things, determined to leave the village unnoticed for the provincial capital. Like a cloud that holds no promise of rain, a swathe of free-flowing water, he must exile himself beyond the horizon.

And yet his feet refuse to obey. Leading to the entrance of the wall encircling the village are three hundred and seventy-two stone steps. He descends three hundred stairs only to retrace two hundred. At this moment, Tiangou is an agitated lion in a zoo pacing back and forth in its cage, a generalissimo in a movie poring over maps on the eve of the final battle.

Eventually, Tiangou makes it to the gate of his Master's house.

秋天 Autumn

"师娘，我来了，我听师傅的!"

正在门口淘米的女人愣住了，极大的震撼使女人承受不了，无知无觉无思无欲地站在那里，米从手缝里流沙似的落下去，突然面部抽搐，泪水涌出，叫一声"天狗!"要从门槛里扑过来，却软在门槛上，只没有字音的无声地哭。

堡子里的干部，族中的长老，还有五里外乡政府的文书，集中在井把式的炕上喝酒。几方对面，承认了这特殊的婚姻。赞同了这三个人组成一个特殊的家庭。当三个指头在一张硬纸上按上红印，瘫子让人扶着靠坐在被子上，把酒敬给众人，敬给天狗，敬给女人，自己也敬自己，咕嘟嘟喝了。

五兴旷了三天学，再一次去上学了。这是天狗的意志，新爹将五兴相送十里，分手了，五兴说："爹，你回去吧。"天狗说："叫叔。"五兴顺从了，再叫一声"叔"，天狗对孩

"Shiniang," he announces, "I'm here. I'll do as Shifu says!"

Rinsing rice by the door, the woman freezes under the sudden shock, unable to feel or perceive, devoid of desire or thought, as rice trickles through her fingers like sand. Suddenly her face contorts and hot tears gush forth.

"Tiangou!" she cries and rushes through the doorway, only to collapse in a heap on the threshold where she weeps in silence, unable to utter a single syllable.

The village officials, clan elders, and a clerk from the township government one-and-a-half-mile away gather at the well-digger's for drinks on the *kang*. Face to face, the delegates acknowledge this unique union and approve the trio's atypical family. Once three fingers have each pressed a crimson print on a thick sheet of paper, the bedridden man requests that he be propped up by a quilt, and then he toasts the guests, Tiangou, the woman, and himself to boot. "*Glug glug,*" down goes the liquor in one go.

For three days Wuxing plays truant, then he heads out for school once again—a firm request on the part of his new Father. Tiangou insists on sending the boy off and only stops after three miles.

"Father," says Wuxing, "please return home now."

"Say 'Uncle'," insists Tiangou.

"Uncle," the boy obeys promptly, winning a genial smile from Tiangou.

秋天 Autumn

子笑笑。

饭桌，别人家都摆在中堂，井把式家的饭桌却是放在炕上的。原先在炕上，现在还在炕上。两个男人，第一个坐在左边，第二个坐在右边，女人不上桌，在灶火口吃饭，一见谁的碗里完了，就双手接过来盛，盛了再双手送过去。

麦田里要浇水，人日夜忙累在地里，吃饭就不在一块了。女人保证每顿饭给第一个煮一个荷包蛋在碗里，第一个却不吃，偷偷夹放在第二个碗底里。天狗回来了，坐在师傅身边吃，吃着吃着，对坐在灶火口的女人说："饭里怎么有个小虫？"把碗放在了锅台上。女人来吃天狗的剩饭，没有发现什么小虫，小虫子变成了那一个荷包蛋。

茶饭慢慢好起来，三个人脸上都有了红润。

几方代表在家喝酒的那天晚上，第一个男人下午就让女人收拾了厦房，糊了顶棚，扫了灰尘，安了床铺，要女人夜

In local courtyards, the dinner table is normally set in the center of the main room. At the well-digger's, a short-legged table is placed atop the *kang*. It was set there before, and remains so. While the two men sit on opposite sides of the table, the woman doesn't take a seat; she eats in front of the earthen stove, where kindling is thrust beneath the wok, and the heat is channelled into the *kang* next to the stove in winter. As soon as she spots an emptied bowl she retrieves it with both hands, and returns it filled, still with both hands.

It is time to irrigate the wheat, and day and night the peasants are toiling in the fields, bent over double. No longer do they eat together. The woman makes sure that a poached egg lies in the bowl for her senior husband at each meal. But he never touches it and quietly stashes the egg at the bottom of the second bowl. When Tiangou comes home later, he sits by Shifu and begins to eat.

"Oh? There's a worm in the rice," he remarks to the woman perched by the stove, and deposits his bowl on the oven top. When she comes to finish his leftovers, there is no worm to be found; it has morphed into an egg.

As the meals gradually improve, all three faces take on a healthy florid complexion.

On that day before the delegates gathered at their house to drink at night, the well-digger had dispatched the woman to prepare the stand-alone hut next to the main dwelling. That

里睡在那里。女人不去。天没黑，第一个男人就将炕上的那个绣了鸳鸯的枕头从窗子丢出去，自个儿裹了被子睡。女人捡了枕头再回来，他举着支窗棍在炕沿上发疯地打。

女人惊惊慌慌地睡在厦房。一夜门没有关。一更里听见了狗咬，起来把门关了；二更里听见院外有走动声，又起来去把门闩抽开，睡在床上睁着眼；三更里夜深沉，只听蛐蛐在墙根鸣叫；四更里迷糊打了个盹；五更里咬着被角无声地哭。天狗他没来。

> 这天狗，想当初，
>
> 精刚刚，虎赳赳，
>
> 一天到晚英武不够。
>
> 自从人招来，
>
> 今日羞，明日愁，

afternoon she pasted new wallpaper on the ceiling, swept the dust, and laid out the bedding. She was to spend the night there, instructed her husband. But she refused.

Before nightfall, the well-digger cast the pillow embroidered with a pair of loving mandarin ducks out the window, and wrapped himself in the quilt to sleep alone on the *kang*. When she retrieved the pillow, he grabbed the stick propping up the window and beat the bed rim like a madman.

Frightened witless, she scurried to the hut to rest, but left the door unbolted. Early in the evening during the first *geng*, she heard dogs barking and got up to close the door; two hours later at the second *geng*, someone walked by their courtyard, so she got up again and undid the latch inside the door before lying down, eyes wide open; in the quiet of midnight, only crickets were heard chirping by the wall; she drifted off briefly in the wee hours of the fourth *geng*; when the fifth *geng* arrived before dawn, silent tears were falling thick and fast, a corner of the quilt clenched in her teeth.

That night, Tiangou never showed.

> *Once upon a time,*
> *Tiangou was tough'n'mighty*
> *like a tiger, day'n'night*
> *gallant as a soldier.*

秋天 Autumn

一下成个泪蜡烛，

蔫得抬不起头。

这女人，想当年，

话不多，眼不乱，

心里好像一条线。

自从招来人，

今日愁，明日羞，

一下成个烂门扇，

日夜合不严。

日月过得平平淡淡、拘拘谨谨。过去的一日不可留，新来的一日又使人愁。又是一次吃罢晚饭，两个男人在炕上吸烟，屋外淅淅沥沥下雨。下了一个时辰，烟袋里的烟末吃完了，天狗站起来，去取柱子上挂着的蓑衣。为大的就说："天狗，你……"天狗装糊涂，说："不早了，你歇下吧，明

Since he entered the house,

he's shy today, forlorn on the morrow,

a weeping shriveled candle,

his head ne'er again held high.

Once upon a time,

the woman had few words and

a steady gaze, her mind

a straight line that never strays.

Since he entered the house,

she's forlorn today, shy on the morrow,

a broken gate never shut

tightly by night or by day.

And thus time sails by uneventfully, with everyone reticent and restrained. While an old day never overstays its welcome, the next ushers in new anxieties.

At the end of another dinner, the two men sit on the *kang*, puffing away at their pipes, raindrops pitter-pattering outside. In two hours of rain, the last bit of tobacco powder in the pouch has turned to smoke and ashes. Tiangou gets up and reaches for the straw rain-cape hanging on the column.

"Tiangou, you..." begins his elder.

"It's getting late, you should rest," says Tiangou, as if

日一早雨还要下，我给咱叫了自乐班来，咱家热闹热闹。"

为大的发了怒，将支窗棍咚地磕在炕沿上，说："你要那样，

我就死在你面前！"天狗木然地立在那里，恭敬得像个儿子，

叫道："师傅……"末了还是默默地走了出去。

雨下得哗哗哗地越发大了。

1992 年

not cottoning on. "It'll rain again early tomorrow morning. I've arranged for an amateur folk opera group to come and liven things up in our household."

This sets off his Shifu. "*Thunk*!" he bangs the wooden window prop against the edge of the *kang*. "You do that," he bellows, "and I'll drop dead right in front of you!"

Tiangou stands there rigid as a column. "Shifu..." he says, full of a son's reverence. Then he turns and walks out in silence.

Outside, the rain pelts down even harder.

1992

制造声音

我去采访这个州刚刚离休的专员。采访结束后我们坐在客厅喝茶，他却放了一段录音问我听到什么，我说是风里的树声。是树声，他说，你听得懂这树声吗？

有树风就有了形状，但风里的树是要说话的。

你知道，这个州是一个贫困的地区，但因处在交通要道

Trees Can Talk!

Translated by Nick Stember

I had come to this city to interview a commissioner, who had just retired. The interview was over, and we were sitting in his living room, drinking tea. He put on a recording and asked what I heard. I told him I heard trees in the wind. "That's right," he said. "Can you understand what the trees are saying?"

Trees give shape to the wind. But trees in the wind can talk.

You know as well as I do that this place is dirt poor. Thanks to all of the roads that pass through here, though, we

上，过往的官员就特别多。我已经是上些岁数的人，实在不宜于干那些恭迎欢送的事，当组织上安排我来，我就想提前离休，或者调往省城寻一个清闲的部门，拈弄笔墨，句读里暗度春光罢了。但到任后的那年秋天，我改变了心态，就一直在州里干了五年。

秋天的这一日，因下乡崴了左脚，在专署里调养，正读一册闲书，上有"留此一双脚，他日小则拜跪上官，胼胝民事；大则跨马据鞍，驰驱天下"句，嘿然而笑，却接到通知：省上又要来一位官员。差不多成了定规，大凡省城、京城来了重要人物，除了布置安全保卫措施，州城的社会环境得治理，卫生得打扫。公安局长就将城中的小商小贩全集中到城南角一条巷中，几条主要街道两旁都摆上了花盆。而一些破烂地段无钱改造，就统统砌了大幅广告。他们在向我汇报时，特意指出已将一个长年在城中上访的疯子用车拉到城

have a long history of officials coming and going.

I'm already well past the age where I should be enjoying big welcomes and send-offs. When they assigned me to this post, my first thought was to take early retirement, or ask for a transfer to an unoccupied governmental position in provincial capital. You know, do some writing, spend my twilight years with my nose in a book. But after what happened the fall after I took office, though, I changed my mind. One thing led to another, and I've already been here for five years now.

What happened was this: I'd sprained my left foot while out on inspection in the countryside, and I was recuperating in my office, doing some light reading, as a matter of fact. I came across the line, "Take care of your feet, so that in youth you may bow before high officials, and serve the people until your feet are callused; and one day, ride a horse and held the reins, traveling to every corner of the land." I couldn't help but laugh out loud.

Just then someone came in to tell me an official was coming to visit from the provincial government.

It's almost a rule now that when someone important visits from the province or the capital, aside from dealing with safety precautions, you have to tidy up things around the city, clean up the streets and so on. The police chief had the peddlers and street sellers moved down to alley at the south end of the city and lined the main streets with flowers. Not having any money to renovate, meanwhile, we covered the worst parts of the city behind big posters. They also reported back that they had

外五十里地方去了，因为这疯子形状肮脏，而且叫嚣省上来了大官他要拦道喊冤哪。

省城的官员到了，他十分地年轻。我的左脚打了封闭针，和地委书记汇报了我们的工作，再听取和认真记录了他的指示，然后陪他参观几个点。那个下午，我们从城南××县回来，才要步行去视察我们的商厦，十字路口那里就拥了一堆人，听得很嘶哑的喊声："树会说话的！树真的会说话的！"我立即知道出了事，脸都气红了，公安局长就跑过来拉我在一旁说，那个疯子谁也没有料到又出现在了城里，而且抱着那电杆拉不走，围观的群众就很多。他向我检讨着他的工作过错，我没时间去训责他，忙鼓动着省上的官员从另一条巷子转过去，但我仍听到那个嘶哑的喊声"树会说话的！树真的……"后边的话"唔"了一下，可能是被手捂住了。地委书记在介绍着那条巷里的明清建筑，我趁机退后，

taken the local eccentric, a persistent petitioner, to a place 50 *li out of the city. He was a dirty, crazy old man, and even worse, he wouldn't stop shouting about some grievance that he* couldn't wait to share with the big wigs who were coming to visit.

When the official from the provincial government arrived, to our surprise, he turned out to be quite young. After getting a shot of anesthetic in my injured left foot, I submitted my progress report to our guest and with the local Party Secretary. We listened closely to his advice, writing down everything. Once we were finished, I suggested that we take him out on a tour. It was afternoon by the time we got back from visiting X County just south of the city. We were walking towards the commercial district when up ahead, at the intersection, we saw that a crowd had gathered. Someone was shouting, "Trees can talk! Trees really can talk!" I knew right away something was up, and my face turned bright red with anger. Just then, the police chief ran up and pulled me aside, letting me know that the crazy old man had found his way back to the city. He'd wrapped his arms around a telephone pole, he said, and he wouldn't let go. Everyone was out for a look. The police chief was trying to apologize, but I didn't have time to bawl him out. I hurriedly steered our visitor in the opposite direction, making a detour through another alley but we still could hear the old man shouting, "Trees can talk! Trees really can... " followed by muffled cry, as if someone had put their hand over his mouth.

招手让公安局长过来，问疯子怎么喊树会说话的？公安局长说，他是为一棵树疯了的，就为一棵树多年在城里上访，满城人没有不认识他的。我说我来这么久了，怎么不知道？公安局长说一个疯子他怎能进了专署大院？我说，你去告诉他，让他不要找省上人，天大的冤枉，晚上到我办公室来说。

晚上，安排了省上官员在宾馆休息后，我虽然累着，但心轻松下来，也并没有睡意，在办公室等待那疯子。左等右等没来，我开始练书法。我这身份不可能去歌舞厅，不可能与人打麻将，下班之后就把自己关在办公室读书练字，我业余唯有这爱好。写了一幅古人句："死之日，以青蝇为吊客；使天下有一人知己，死不恨。"公安局长就亲自坐车把疯子拉了来。疯子竟是下午被关进了拘留所的，我对公安局长大为光火，并且赔情道歉。疯子是一个七十岁左右的老头，个子

Later, while the Party Secretary introduced a row of buildings, some of which dated back to the Ming and Qing dynasties, I held back, gesturing for the police chief to come over. "Why was the crazy old man shouting that trees could talk?" I asked. He said it was all about some old tree in his village. He had been appealing to authorities about his tree for years. Everyone here knew about the old man and his tree. I asked, "How come I don't, when I've been here so long?" "A deranged old man like that? In your office?" I said, "Go tell him that he doesn't need to go looking for officials from the province and making his case out to be bigger than it is. No matter how big his grievance is, tell him to come and visit my office tonight."

That evening I dropped off our guest in his hotel to rest. Even though I was tired, I wasn't angry anymore and didn't feel much like going to sleep. Instead, I went to my office to wait for the old man. After a long time with no sign of him, I took out my brush and ink to practice my calligraphy. As commissioner, it wouldn't do for me to be seen going out dancing or playing mahjong. So after work, I had developed the habit of locking myself up in the office to read and practice calligraphy. Those are my only hobbies. I once wrote out a famous line: "On my last day, flies will serve as funeral guests; I'll die without regret only if one man knows me well."
The old man arrived not long after, personally escorted by the police chief. It turned out that he had spent the afternoon locked up. I made my displeasure clear to the police chief and

高大，但枯瘦如柴，头发和胡子已成毡片，浑身散发着一股难闻的酸臭味。老头进拘留所似乎并未介意，对公安局长的道歉也无动于衷，只嚷道："树会说话的！树是一九四八年栽的！"公安局长说："你嚷什么呀？这是专员！"老头说："专员，树会说话的！"公安局长就吓唬了："你再嚷？！"老头偏梗着脖子，脖子上暴起了几条青筋说："树就是会说话的！"我说："好吧，树会说话的。"老头得意地看了公安局长一眼，一颗清涕就吊在鼻尖，一把捏下来要揩向桌腿，后来还是揩在身上的裤腰处。我让他坐，他说他不坐，公安局长说："让你坐你就坐！"按他在椅子上。我摆摆手让公安局长出去，开始询问老头。

你叫什么名字？

杨二娃。

哪个县里的？

××县××乡东洼村。

多大岁数了？

不大，才七十还差十天。

你有什么冤枉事？

he apologized to the old man, who looked to be around seventy years old. He was tall and skinny, as withered as old firewood. His long hair and wild beard had grown together into a single mat, and he reeked of sweat. He didn't seem to care about being thrown in jail, and he completely ignored the police chief's apology. Instead, he shouted, "Trees can talk! The tree says it was planted in 1948!" The police chief said, "What's all that hollering? This is the commissioner!" The old man said, "Commissioner, the tree can talk!" The police chief gave him a threatening look. "This again?!" The old man thrust out his neck, the veins practically popping out. "Trees really can talk!" I said, "Fine, fine, trees can talk." The old man glared triumphantly at the police chief. He wiped at a blob of snot dangling from the tip of his nose, and made to brush it off on the table leg. Thinking better of it, he rubbed it on the seat of his pants. I invited him to sit, but he refused. The police chief said, "The commissioner wasn't asking!" Taking him by the shoulders, he pushed him into the chair. I waved my hand, gesturing for the police chief to leave before I continued my questions.

"What's your name?"

"Yang Erwa."

"What county?"

"X County, Y Township, East Hollow Village."

树是一九四八年栽的，不是一九五二年栽的。怎么能是一九五二年呢？不是一九五二年，是一九四八年。树会说话的。

就为这事吗？

就为这事。

你告了多少年了？

十五年零三个月。

为一棵树值得告十五年？

可树就是一九四八年栽的，为什么要说是一九五二年栽的？

这点事村里就可以解决嘛！

德贵是坏人！

德贵是谁？

村长。他谋算这棵树哩，他想收回去再买了给他多做棺材的。

你找过乡长吗？

人家在一个壶里尿！

一个壶里尿？

德贵的婆娘是个卖×的，她和乡长……

住嘴！你怎么这样骂人？

"How old are you?"

"Not old at all, ten days to seventy."

"What's your grievance?"

"The tree was planted in 1948, not 1952. How could it be 1952? It wasn't planted in 1952, it was planted in 1948. The tree can talk."

"Is that it?"

"That's it."

"How long have you been trying to get your case heard?"

"Fifteen years and three months."

"All that for a tree?"

"But the tree was planted in 1948, why would they say it was planted in 1952?"

"Your village should be able to handle a case like this!"

"It's all Degui's fault!"

"Who's Degui?"

"The village head. He has his eye on the tree. Wants to cut it down so he can make a coffin for his father."

"Did you talk it over with the township head?"

"They piss in the same pot!"

"Piss in the same pot?"

"Degui's wife is a whore, she and the township head..."

"That's enough! How can you curse people like that?"

"Okay, okay. I won't curse them anymore."

我不骂了。

你说吧。

乡长我找过三十二次，他派人打我，我到县上去，县上的"父母官"我都找过，"父母官"两年就换了人。张县长说要解决，但他调走了。又来了陆县长，他让乡里解决，乡里不解决，向上反映我是刁民。我不是刁民。我又找刘县长，王县长，马县长，他们都不理我了，说我是疯子。我是疯子吗？

不是疯子。

不是疯子！树是一九四八年栽的就是一九四八年栽的，我要是疯子我能记得树是一九四八年栽的？

你说树是一九四八年栽的，那树还在吗？

在的。它今年老了，身上有一个洞，东边那个枝丫枯了，那原先上边有个鸟窠的，八月初三的夜里刮风，窠就掉下来，这窠应该归我的，村长的儿子却捡了去，那是能做三天饭的柴火哩，我去……

你说树是一九四八年栽的，你有什么证明？

"Go on then. "

"I've talked to the township head thirty-two times. He finally sent his thugs to beat me up. I came to the county seat, and I talked to all the ' local magistrates ' but they get transferred every two years. County Head Zhang said he'd take care of it but he got transferred. County Head Lu came next, but he said it was a matter for the township, not the county. But the township wouldn't take the case. They got me written up as a troublemaker. I'm no troublemaker. I talked to County Head Liu, County Head Wang, County Head Ma, but none of them would listen to me. They all said I was crazy. Am I crazy?"

"You're not crazy. "

"I'm not! If a tree is planted in 1948, then it was planted in 1948. If I'm crazy, how come I can remember when the tree was planted?"

"The tree that you say was planted in 1948, is it still there?"

"Sure. He's getting old now though. He's got holes in him, and the branch on the east side is withered and dead. There used to be a bird nest up there, but a windstorm on that night—on the third day of the eighth lunar month—knocked it out. That should have been mine, but the village chief's son picked it up. Three days of kindling, f**k... "

"You said the tree was planted in 1948. Do you have any

我老婆证明。一九四八年春上我和我老婆去她娘家当天回来我栽的，栽了树老婆给我擀的宽片杂面，调的干辣面，没有盐的，老婆说你将就将就吃。

那你老婆怎么不出来证明？

她死了。这娘们儿害了我一辈子，该她作证的时候，她就上吊死了！这狗娘们儿，她死了我懒得给她烧倒头纸，别人家的老婆都是帮夫运，她却猪一样要我养活！

还有什么证明？

拴狗那老能证明。我栽树时他正在地头捡粪哩，但他瞧别人都是说树是一九五二年栽的，他就说他记不住陈年老事了。拴狗老我瞧不起他！没人作证，可树会说话呀，他们就是不去听！

家里还有什么人？

一个儿子，死了。儿子是好儿子。他像我，村人都说我们是一个模子倒出来的。儿子陪我去县上上访，回来搭的拖拉机，拖拉机翻了，我没事，拖拉机却压在他肚子上，肠子就压了出

proof?"

"My wife can prove it. In the spring of 1948, my wife and I went to her mom's village. I planted it after we came back. After I planted it, my wife made wide noodle stew, with chili and no salt. My wife said you just have to make do."

"How come your wife didn't come and testify?"

"She's dead. Life-long pain in the neck is what she is! Just when I need her, she goes and hangs herself! After the bitch killed herself, I couldn't be bothered to burn any paper for her. Other people's wives help out around the house and bring good luck to their husbands. But all she ever did was wait around to get fed like a pig in shit."

"Do you have any other proof?"

"The man with the dog can testify. When I was planting the tree, he was out collecting shit. But when he heard everybody else was saying the tree was planted in 1952, he claimed he couldn't remember stuff from way back when like that. F**k the dog man! No one will back me up, but trees can talk. People just won't listen!"

"Is there anyone else in your family?"

"My son, but he's dead too. He was a good son. He was the spitting image of me, everyone in the village says so. My son came with me to the county to try my case. We took a tractor back. The tractor flipped. I was fine, but the tractor

来。我那老婆向我要儿子，我骂了她，她就死在绳上的。

嗯。

专员，树肯定是一九四八年栽的，不是一九五二年栽的，你去听听，树会说话的。

杨二娃——

在的。

就这样吧。你拿上这点钱，明日去车站买了票回去。不要再跑了。我派人很快去给你落实，是一九四八年栽的就是一九四八年栽的，是一九五二年栽的就是一九五二年栽的，我给你个结果。

是一九四八年栽的！如果你们硬要说不是一九四八年栽的，我还要告的。你叫什么名字？

惠世清。

那好。那我就告德贵，乡长，王县长张县长陆县长刘县长马县长，还有你惠世清，惠专员！

送走了省上的官员，我打电话给××县的马县长，托他

landed on my son's stomach and pushed his guts out. When my wife asked where our son was, I cursed her and she hung herself."

"Huh."

"Commissioner, I'm certain the tree was planted in 1948, not 1952. Just go and listen, trees can talk."

"Yang Erwa—"

"Uh-huh."

"Here's what we're going to do. Take this money, go to the station tomorrow and buy a ticket home. Don't go running around again. I'll send a team to find out the truth. If the tree was planted in 1948, then it was planted in 1948. If it was planted in 1952, then it was planted in 1952. Either way, we'll let you know."

"But the tree was planted in 1948! If you end up deciding the tree was planted in 1952, I'm not giving up. What's your name?"

"Hui Shiqing."

"Fine. I'll sue you all. Village Head Degui, Township Head, County Head Wang, County Head Zhang, County Head Lu, County Head Liu, County Head Ma, and you, Hui Shiqing. Commissioner Hui!"

After I'd seen off our guest from the provincial government, I called County Head Ma in X County and asked him to send me Yang Erwa's police record. County Head Ma

把有关杨二娃的档案材料送上来。马县长亲自来州城向我汇报，杨二娃竟没有什么档案材料，但马县长知道这件事，说这棵树是在东洼村南头，树下的那块地新中国成立前属杨二娃的地，新中国成立后土地收公，树却归私人。那时树小，谁也没在意，后来树大了，杨二娃说树是一九四八年栽的，树权归他私人，村里人说树是一九五二年栽的，一九五二年栽在地头的树应归村里。村里每年要伐，杨二娃都护树，他把旧屋拆了重新盖在树下，现在树身就长在屋当堂里。

就为这棵树，能值几个钱？马县长说，农民爱认死理，杨二娃疯疯癫癫告了十五年，活得真没个意思！

那你说，怎么活着有意思呢？

我训斥着我的部下，命令他们组织个专案组，去东洼村落实这件事，树是有年轮的，可以请一些专家考证一下树到底是一九四八年的还是一九五二年的。

personally came to deliver his report. He said Yang Erwa didn't have a police record, but he was familiar with his case. He said the tree was located on the south side of East Hollow Village. The land it was on belonged to Yang Erwa before New China was established in 1949. The land became public property during the land reforms, but any trees on it would have remained private property. When the tree was still small nobody paid it much mind. But later, when the tree had grown up, Yang Erwa said it was planted in 1948, so it belonged to him. The other villagers said it was planted in 1952, on public land, so it should belong to the village. The long and short of it was, they had been trying to cut it down for years, but Yang Erwa always found a way to save it at the last minute. He even tore down his house and rebuilt so that the tree was now standing right in his living room.

"How much can a tree like that be worth?" County Head Ma said, "Farmers are pig-headed like that. Crazy old Yang Erwa has been trying to get his case heard for fifteen years now. Not a very meaningful life if you ask me."

"I suppose you can tell me what is?"

After chewing out my subordinates, I ordered them to put together a task force to resolve the case in East Hollow Village. "Trees have growth rings," I said. "Invite some experts to tell you whether the tree was planted in 1948 or 1952."

专案组很快就回来了，考证出树是一九四八年栽的。我做了批示：树归属于杨二娃。

这件事就这样结束了。

第二年春天，××县旱象严重，我下去检查灾情，突然想起了杨二娃和那棵一九四八年栽下的树。我和马县长坐车往东洼村，打问杨二娃，村人说，杨二娃吗，早死了！

杨二娃死了。这老头瘦是瘦，精神头儿还好，而树被断定为一九四八年栽的，又归属于他，冬天里他就病倒了。一开春，地气上升，病又加重，不知什么时候咽气在家里，村人发现了的时候，人已经僵硬。

马县长说，这老头，他要是继续上访，可能还要活着。

马县长的话是对的，这么说，是我害死了这老头。

(嘻)，朝闻道，夕死可矣，这是孔子说的吧？马县长指着一个小虫子，小虫子是从树上吊一条丝下来的，但小虫子

It wasn't long before the task force came back. They concluded that the tree was planted in 1948. In my memorandum I wrote:

The tree belongs to Yang Erwa.

And that was the end of the whole business. Or so I thought.

The next spring, X County was suffering from a serious drought, and I went out to the countryside to assess the situation. That was when I remembered Yang Erwa and the tree he planted in 1948. County Head Ma and I drove to East Hollow Village, and asked about Yang Erwa. The villagers said, "You haven't heard?"

That was when I learned that Yang Erwa had died. Skinny as he was, the old man had seemed to get around okay. But after we announced that the tree was planted in 1948 and it belonged to him, he went home, and fell ill that winter. It was a damp spring, and he only got worse. He died in bed, but nobody could say for sure when. By the time the villagers had found him he was already stiff.

County Head Ma said, "If he had kept trying his case, he might still be alive."

If that was true, then it meant I killed the old man.

I sighed. "If a man learns the Way in the morning, he can die without regret in the evening. Isn't that what Confucius said?" County Head Ma pointed at a dead caterpillar hanging

是死的：这小虫子也闻道了！

这树要是不断定为一九四八年栽的，老头就一百年一千年地活下去吗？

树依然活着，树是常见的那种椿树，确是老得身上有了洞，除了东边的枝丫枯了，西边的枝丫也枯了，树身三分之一在一间歪歪斜斜的屋子中间。杨二娃因是孤人，死后村人就以他家的柜做了棺材，在屋中掘坑下葬，这房子也锁了门，让它自废自塌了将来就是坟丘。

我说，给老头奠奠酒吧。

秘书去买了一瓶酒，我就把酒全浇在屋前。这时起了风，风是看不见的，但椿树枝叶摇摆，嘎嘎作响，风就有了形状，树也有了声。老头给我说过树会说话的，树会说什么话呢？我听不出来，便用录音机录了。

多少年里，我一直在企图听懂这树声，你听听，这树在说的什么话呢？

1998 年

by a thread from the tree and said, "I suppose this little bug knows the Way then!"

If we hadn't set the record straight about the tree being planted in 1948... who's to say? Maybe he would have lived to one hundred, or one thousand?

The tree was still alive. It was just a common sumac, but like the old man had said, there were holes in its trunk, and the east branch was withered and dead. Now the west branch was gone, too. The bottom third of the tree disappeared into a crooked-looking shack. Since Yang Erwa didn't have any family, the villagers buried him in the floor of the shack, with an old cupboard as a coffin. They locked the door and left the shack to fall apart—a tomb of his own.

I said, "Let's pour the old man a drink."

The secretary bought me a bottle, and I emptied it out on the ground in front of his makeshift tomb. The wind picked up. You couldn't see it, but the leaves and branches of the sumac whispered and rustled, giving shape to the wind, talking in the wind. The old man had told me that trees can talk. But what would they say if they could? I couldn't make it out, so I used a tape recorder to make this recording.

I've been trying for years. Tell me, what do you think the tree is saying?

1998

猎　人

戚子绍在礼拜五的下午去秦岭打猎时要带上一个叫夏清
的女子，王老板问是不是情人，戚子绍说才认识的，应该是
熟人，女熟人。王老板就认为打猎带女人不好，又累又不安
全，而且三天里住宿也不方便。戚子绍噎了一句："你舍不

The Hunter

Translated by Annelise Finegan Wasmoen

On the Friday afternoon Qi Zishao went hunting in the Qin Mountains, he planned to bring along a woman named Xia Qing. Mr. Wang, a businessman, asked if they were lovers. Qi Zishao said they had met only recently so she counted as an acquaintance, a female friend. Mr. Wang didn't think taking women hunting was a good idea. It was exhausting and dangerous, and finding lodgings for three nights would be difficult. Qi Zishao cut him off: "Are you afraid of spending

得花钱了?!"王老板便不再嘟囔,将车开到 A 路 B 楼外的花坛边按喇叭,一长一短地按得生响。楼道里跑出来的却是两个女人,打头儿的是个胖子,四肢短短的,跑起来像是鸭子。戚子绍迎着阳光,把眉头皱成一疙瘩,等胖子跑过来了,一边替夏清拿了大包小包,一边却对着胖子笑。

"怎么个给你拨电话也联系不上!我还担心你不能去呢!"戚子绍说。

"怕不是吧,"胖子做着鬼脸。胖子做鬼脸的时候很性感。"认识了夏清就不想见我了?这我知道。可我和夏清是笼沿连着笼襻儿,不拆伴的!"

夏清站在车尾,抿着嘴笑,戚子绍又一次笑了。

"我怀疑你俩是同性恋!"

"或许是吧!"

王老板已经把车门打开,胖子的一只腿伸出去,又取出

money?" Mr. Wang stopped grumbling and brought his jeep around to the flowerbed in front of Building B alongside Road A, where he pressed down on the horn, one long beep and one short. Two women hurried out of the passageway. The first was fat with stubby limbs that made her look like a duck as she ran. Qi Zishao stared up at the sun, wrinkling his forehead and waiting for her to reach the jeep before he helped Xia Qing behind her carry their various bags, all the while simpering at the chubby woman.

"I phoned, but I couldn't get through. I was worried you weren't coming!" Qi Zishao said.

"No, you weren't," Chubby pulled a funny face, which made her look sexy. "Now that you've met Xia Qing you don't want to see me anymore, I know. But we're inseparable, you can't have one without the other."

Xia Qing was standing behind the car with a close-lipped smile. Qi Zishao laughed again.

"I suspected you were lesbians!"

"Maybe we are!"

Mr. Wang had already opened the car door. Chubby put one leg in and pulled it back out with a cry of surprise as she

来，哇地叫了一下，瞧见了装在里边的长舌帽、爬山鞋、军用水壶、雨伞、毛毯、一袋子矿泉水和三支长长短短的猎枪。说："戚处长，你还真的是个猎人了！"

"干啥就要像啥嘛！"戚子绍在后车厢帮夏清将一个大旅行袋放好，这是一顶军用的野营帐篷。戚子绍低声说："是你通知了她？"夏清说："你打电话过来时她就在旁边，我不能瞒了她。"戚子绍说："傻女子！"夏清说："我是傻。"蓝底碎白花的裙子在阳光下一抖，戚子绍觉得满地都是坠落的花瓣了。胖子在问王老板："这是你的三菱吉普？多有个性的车，我就喜欢红颜色的！"王老板说："是小了点，但爬山功能好。"戚子绍关了后车厢盖，悄悄说："他是我的客户。"揩了夏清手背上的一点土，夏清忙把手塞进了口袋里，戚子绍却冲了胖子说："车不错吧，老王可是个大老板喽！"胖子说："你净结识大老板！"戚子绍说："也结识美女呀！"走到

caught sight of the three hunting rifles of different lengths bundled among hunting caps, hiking boots, army canteens, umbrellas, blankets, and a sack of mineral water. She said, "Director Qi, you really are a hunter!"

"You have to look the part!" Qi Zishao was helping Xia Qing load a large travel bag holding an army tent in the trunk. He lowered his voice: "Were you the one who told her?" Xia Qing said, "She was with me when you phoned, I couldn't keep her in the dark." Qi Zishao said, "Stupid girl!" Xia Qing said, "I am stupid." Her blue skirt with its white floral pattern fluttered in the sunlight, and Qi Zishao imagined the whole earth covered with falling petals. Chubby was asking Mr. Wang, "Is this your Mitsubishi? It has a lot of personality, I like this red." Mr. Wang replied, "It's a little small, but it comes in handy for driving in the mountains." Qi Zishao shut the trunk and said quietly, "He's one of my clients." He brushed a speck of dirt from the back of Xia Qing's hand and she hurriedly stuffed her hands into her pockets. Qi Zishao turned to Chubby: "It's a good car. Old Wang's an important businessman!" Chubby said, "You only know important businessmen!" Qi Zishao said: "And beautiful

前面，为胖子拉开车门，很绅士地说："请!"胖子却说："是要我坐在前边，你们坐后边哪？我也偏坐在后边!"把吃的喝的用的东西，往前边座位上堆，堆成一个小山。

"不愿意我坐后边?"胖子让戚子绍坐在后座位的中间了，自己挤进来。戚子绍说："这盼不得吗，东宫西宫，我过的是皇帝生活嘛!"故意摇晃着身子，将手在胖子的膝盖上拍了一下，便问："最近做啥哩?"胖子说："啥也没做，只做爱。"四个人都噗地笑了，戚子绍说："这话说得好! 王老板，你瞧我这女熟人有意思吧?"胖子说："我可告诉你，下次再出来玩不首先通知我，我会生气的。你要待我好些，我可以继续给你批发美人，我是胖了点，我的女朋友却没有不漂亮的!"

戚子绍确实是先认识了胖子，然后通过胖子认识了夏清的。那日他在一个朋友家搓麻将，麻将桌上有胖子，她是一

women!" He stepped chivalrously to the front of the car and held the door open: "After you!" But Chubby said, "Am I supposed to sit in front, while you two sit in the back? I want to sit in back, too." She shifted the food, drinks, and equipment into the front seat, heaping them into a mound.

"So you don't want me to sit in back?" Chubby made Qi Zishao sit in the middle, and squeezed herself into the seat. Qi Zishao said: "An unexpected pleasure: I'm like an emperor with my empress on one side and concubine on the other!" He deliberately rocked from side to side and put a hand on Chubby's knee: "What have you been up to recently?" Chubby: "Nothing, just making love." The four of them guffawed, and Qi Zishao replied: "Well put! Mr. Wang, you see how much fun my female friends are?" Chubby: "Listen to me, next time you go out and don't call me first, I'll be angry. You should treat me better so I can keep supplying you with wholesale beauties. Maybe I'm a little fat, but all of my friends are pretty!"

Qi Zishao had met Chubby first, then later on she had introduced him to Xia Qing. One day he had gone to a friend's house to play mahjong and Chubby was sitting at the playing

The Hunter
猎
人

家公司的职员，询问他们银行能不能采用她经销的 UPS 不间断电源器，这是微机上使用的配件，一旦使用上了就能长期使用。"这有什么问题呀，"戚子绍是当场拍了腔子，"用谁的配件都是用，辞掉别的供货用你们的就是了！"但过后他却没有动静。有一天胖子又来了，领着的是夏清，夏清是一个瘦高瘦高的女子，戚子绍就有些拘谨。戚子绍是见着了漂亮的女人就拘谨的。"你是上海来的?"他舌头硬硬地说了普通话。女人说："鄂不是。"一听把我念成"鄂"，戚子绍才知道夏清是本城人，他就说西安还能有这么漂亮的女人呀，而且气质好。那天戚子绍说了许多话，都很幽默，简直是妙语连珠，胖子说你爱上她了? 他说，哪里? 胖子说，这你瞒不了我的感觉，瞧你想象力多好！第二天戚子绍就约了夏清去茶楼吃茶，夏清应约而来，来的还有胖子。戚子绍是有了许多话想要给夏清说，但胖子老在旁边，她们总是一块来一

table. She had asked whether the bank where he worked could use the Uninterruptible Power Supply she was selling on commission, a device that provided backup power for microprocessors and could be used long-term. "No problem at all," Qi Zishao slapped his chest. "It doesn't matter whose accessories they are—let's get rid of the other supplier and use yours!" She hadn't heard from him afterward. One day Chubby was there again, and she brought along Xia Qing. Xia Qing was tall and slender and Qi Zishao became reserved, as he always did when he met a beautiful woman. "Are you from Shanghai?" he asked, his tongue stiff at speaking the standard Chinese. The woman said: "E'm not." The moment he heard her say "E'm" instead of "I'm," he knew she was a native of Xi'an. He said, "Who knew Xi'an had such beautiful, such chic women?" That day he talked a great deal, a deluge of witticisms, until Chubby said, "Are you in love with her?" He said: "No." Chubby said: "You can't hide things from me, don't imagine you can!" Qi Zishao made an appointment to see Xia Qing at a teahouse the next day. She came as arranged, and Chubby came along, too. There were many things Qi Zishao wanted to say to Xia Qing, but Chubby was constantly

块去，戚子绍没有了机会，但戚子绍还是帮忙推销了。

秦岭在城南五十里外，车行驶了半小时，进了沣峪口，路就在峡谷的半崖上蜿蜒盘旋，每每车在拐弯处就倾斜，坐在座位中间的戚子绍就一会靠在胖子的身上，一会挤着了夏清，夏清被挤得嗷嗷地叫。戚子绍说："这是身子要倒的，与道德品质无关啊！"头与头要挨上的时候，戚子绍瞧着夏清的眼睛说贴这么长的睫毛，夏清说不是贴的，戚子绍用手去拔了一下，果然不是贴的，就感叹什么叫天生丽质。王老板故意把车开得很猛，三个人就颠得像在舞蹈，戚子绍就势用双臂搂住夏清和胖子，却叮咛王老板把反光镜拧上去，专心开车。王老板真的把反光镜拧了上去，声明他不会看的，他什么都没看见，就听着他们在后边说女人的高跟鞋和香水，戚子绍的观点是高跟鞋是世界上最伟大的一项发明，但香水却破坏了女人特有的体味。这话惹得胖子坚决反对，因

at her side. They always arrived and left together, giving Qi Zishao no chance. He still helped out with Chubby's UPS sale.

The Qin Mountains were twenty-five kilometers south of the city. After driving half an hour, they reached the entrance to the Feng Ravine, where the road wound and zigzagged halfway up the side of a canyon. The jeep lurched around the bends and in the middle of the backseat Qi Zishao was pressed one moment against Chubby and the next moment against Xia Qing. Xia Qing was crowded so hard she yelped in pain. Qi Zishao said: "I can't help falling into you, it has nothing to do with my morals!" When their heads were thrown together Qi Zishao looked into Xia Qing's eyes and said, "You've stuck on such long eyelashes." Xia Qing said they weren't stick-ons. Qi Zishao brushed them with his hand. They really weren't, and he exclaimed, "This is what 'natural beauty' means!" Mr. Wang's driving was deliberately wild and the three of them jostled around as if they were dancing. Qi Zishao used the momentum to his advantage and embraced Xia Qing and Chubby, one in each arm, while he urged Mr. Wang to adjust the inside rear-view mirror and concentrate on his driving. Mr. Wang fixed the mirror and announced that he wasn't looking at them, he couldn't see anything at all. He could still hear them in the backseat talking about high heels and perfume. Qi

为她今天没有穿高跟鞋而喷洒了强烈的香水。夏清即将双腿收缩在身下。戚子绍也就说了一句胖子的丝袜好，丝袜是女人的第二层皮肤。胖子说："只许看不许摸！你们常进山打猎吗？"戚子绍说："当然喽，差不多的礼拜都来！"胖子说："有钱有权的人真会生活！政府不是禁止民间有枪吗，你长长短短三支枪？"戚子绍说："这办了许可证啊！你需要办不？我可以帮你办一张。"王老板说："这可是真的，在西安市里戚处长没有什么事情他搞不定的！"夏清说："这我信的，你就是要颗原子弹，戚处长就说你要圆头的还是方头的。"车突然地一个急刹，胖子和夏清从座位上滚下去，而戚子绍一个前倾头撞在了前边的椅背上，"哎哟"叫了一声。一辆车从拐弯的对面擦身而过，在后面发出了剧烈的机器响。戚子绍脸色愠怒，随之解嘲说："王老板你是牺牲我呀？！瞧见了吗，刚才那辆车上坐着一位少妇！"

Zishao's position was that high heels were the greatest invention in the world, whereas perfume ruined the characteristic smell of a woman's body. This provoked Chubby into firm opposition, because she had not worn heels today, but had sprayed on a strong perfume. Xia Qing promptly gathered both of her feet underneath her. Qi Zishao complimented Chubby's silk stockings, saying stockings were a woman's second layer of skin. Chubby said: "You can look but you can't touch! Do you often go hunting in the mountains?" Qi Zishao said: "Of course, we go hunting most weekends." Chubby said: "Men with money and power know how to enjoy the good life! Isn't it illegal for ordinary citizens to have guns? Where did you get your rifles—three altogether?" Qi Zishao said: "They're licensed. Would you like a license? I could help you get one." Mr. Wang said: "It's true, there's nothing Director Qi can't make happen in Xi'an!" Xia Qing said: "I can believe it. If you wanted an atomic bomb, Director Qi would ask if you needed it with a round or a square warhead." The jeep braked hard. Chubby and Xia Qing tumbled down off the seat, but Qi Zishao was leaning forward so his head struck the back of the seat in front of him and he shouted in pain. A car in the opposite lane scraped past them around a curve in the road, followed by a violent mechanical sound. Qi Zishao excused his temper with a

"你眼睛那么尖的?"胖子重新坐好,但她的丝袜被座位上的硬垫角剐破了。

"这就是猎人的眼睛!"戚子绍说,"看女人瞥一眼就知道什么模样了!那少妇倒有些姿色。"

三个人扭过头了,看见那辆车在后边二十米远停住,先是司机下来查看轮胎,接着是一个女人也下来,腰身很好,但脸是刀把脸。两个女人同时地"噢"了一声,汽车也已转过了弯道。

"戚处长是这样个欣赏水平呀?!"

戚子绍似乎也不好意思了,从前边的座位上拿起了一支枪,向窗外做着瞄准的姿势。

"我是侧面看她的,"戚子绍说,"侧面看想犯罪,正面看了想自卫。"

"我现在也不能不怀疑你的枪法了。"胖子说。

joke, "Mr. Wang, are you trying to sacrifice me? Did you see the young woman in that car?"

"Are your eyes really that sharp?" Chubby regained her seat. Her stockings had torn on the hard corner of the seat cushion.

"I have the eyes of a hunter," Qi Zishao said. "I can tell everything about a woman just by a fleeting glance. And she was worth looking at!"

Three heads turned and they saw that the other car had come to a stop some twenty meters behind them. First the driver got out to examine the tires, followed by a woman. Her figure was nice, but she had a long face like a knife-handle. The two women said "oh" at the same time, and the jeep turned a bend in the road.

"Director Qi, is that the type you like?"

Qi Zishao seemed embarrassed. He picked up a rifle from the front seat and posed aiming it out the window.

"I saw her from the side," he said, "and she made me want to commit a crime, but when I saw her face I thought I would have to defend myself."

"Now I can't help doubting your aim," Chubby said.

The Hunter
猎
人

"可以说，来秦岭打猎的没有谁能和我比枪法的！"戚子绍说，"我曾经一枪打下两只鸟的！"

"是两只鸟，"王老板做证，"鸟落了一树，一枪放上去，掉下来了一只，过一会，又掉下来了一只。"

"第二只是吓昏了的吧。"夏清说。

"不打鸟而让鸟掉下来才是高手！"戚子绍说。

两个女人却听不懂这样的话，相视着咯咯地笑。

"你瞧着吧，这次打猎我不往崖鸡子身上打一枪，却要猎到十只八条的！"

两个女人还是在笑。

戚子绍就给女人讲他和王老板上次猎崖鸡子的经历，如何潜伏在一个土沟里，看着对面崖畔上落着一群崖鸡子，咚地朝天放一枪，崖鸡子就扑棱棱地起飞了，飞过沟就落在这畔上，咚地朝天又是一枪，崖鸡子又飞落到那边崖畔上。

"There's no one hunting in the Qin Mountains who is as good a marksman as me," Qi Zishao said. "I once downed two birds with a single bullet!"

"Two birds," Mr. Wang confirmed. "They landed in a tree, he fired and one bird fell to the ground, then a second bird dropped out of the tree."

"The second one was frightened and it fainted, huh?" Xia Qing said.

"It takes a real expert to bring down a bird without hitting it!" Qi Zishao said. The two women didn't understand, so they looked at each other and tittered.

"Watch me, this time I'll bag eight or ten pheasants without even shooting directly at them!"

The women kept laughing.

Qi Zishao told them about the last time he and Mr. Wang had gone hunting for mountain pheasants. How they had hidden in a gully, watching a flock come to rest on the opposite side of the cliff. Boom! They shot into the air and the pheasants flapped their wings and flew across the gully, landing on this side of the cliff. Boom! Another shot into the air, and the pheasants flew back to the other side of the cliff.

"崖鸡子是没脑子的，就像是夏清。"戚子绍趁机敲了一下夏清的鼻子，夏清回击了，捏了戚子绍的鼻子。戚子绍的鼻子被捏得发红，他继续说，他和王老板不停地朝天放枪，崖鸡子就不停地飞过来又飞过去，崖鸡就累死了，接二连三地从空中像石头一样掉下来。

"哦。"

两个女人终于相信戚子绍是个猎人，一个真正的猎人了。

车愈往秦岭的深处去，景色愈好，山有开有合，云忽聚忽散，两个女人兴奋不已，后悔着从来没有进过深山，这般好的去处，住十天八天也不想回城了。戚子绍说："那就不回去了，咱们就住在山里，到时候咱们六个人……"胖子说："四个人怎么成了六个人？"戚子绍说："那还有孩子呀！"胖子说："想了个美！"车从一个隧道里穿过去，一阵

"Mountain pheasants have no brains, just like Xia Qing." Qi Zishao rapped Xia Qing on the nose. She countered with a pinch. Red-nosed, he went on to tell them about how he and Mr. Wang continued shooting into the air and the pheasants kept flying over and back until one after another they died of exhaustion and fell from the sky like stones.

"Oh."

The two women were finally convinced that Qi Zishao was a hunter, a proper hunter.

As the jeep progressed deeper into the Qin Mountains, the scenery became more spectacular. The mountains closed in around them and opened up again; the clouds gathered and dispersed. The two women were endlessly excited, wondering why they had never driven into the mountains before. It was an excellent place to visit—they should stay the whole next week instead of returning to the city. Qi Zishao said, "Let's not go back then. We'll live in the mountains, and when the time comes the six of us will..." Chubby interrupted, "How are you getting six from the four of us?" Qi Zishao said, "There are also the children!" Chubby said: "What an idea!" The jeep drove through a tunnel and after a stretch of darkness arrived

黑暗，隧洞外是一个小的山村。

山村河的这边有几户人家，河的那边有几户人家，河这边的人家除了路边高高地架着皮管子接引了山泉里的水，为过往车辆冲洗外，又都开着饭馆。洞开的土窗外挂着酱黑色的腊肉、干蕨菜和酱条串成的卤汁豆腐干，卖饭的男人或女人圪蹴在门口的石头上。刚才车到的时候，一个肥胖的女人从厕所里出来，站在公路中间，一边系裤带一边乍了一下腿，车就地停了。肥胖女人趴住车窗往里一看，就乐了。

"是戚处长呀，不挡车你还不停哩？又来打崖鸡子啊！"

"打崖鸡子！"

"守着凤凰还要崖鸡子呀？"

"凤凰只能看不能吃嘛！是漂亮吧？"

"漂亮得像是狐狸变的。"

夏清低声说了："你是猪托生的！"下了车和胖子看这看

at a small mountain village on the other side.

The village was a handful of houses on each side of the river. The people on the near side of the river had set rubber pipes high above the roadside, channeling water down from a mountain spring to wash cars passing through. There were also restaurants with black soy-marinated meat, dried fernbrake, and strips of dried bean curd hung in bunches from windows cut into earth walls. The men and women who sold the food squatted on stones in their doorways. Just as the jeep drove up, an obese woman came out of the latrine and stood in the middle of the road, tying her belt with her legs spread apart as the vehicle came to a halt. The large woman leaned into the window, looked inside, and laughed.

"It's Director Qi! Were you going to stop if I hadn't gotten in the way? Are you here to hunt pheasants again?"

"Yes, mountain pheasants!"

"You have a phoenix here and you still want pheasants?"

"I can only look at the phoenix, not eat her! She's too pretty!"

"So pretty she might be a fox spirit transformed."

Xia Qing lowered her voice, "And you're a pig reincarnated!" She got out of the jeep to look around with Chubby, finding everything novel and curious. Qi Zishao, who

那，看啥都稀奇。戚子绍觉得很得意，提醒着山里路不平，走路脚要抬高点，继续和肥胖女人搭讪："近来打猎的多不多？"

"来得少了，你不知道吧，山顶上有了狗熊啦！都怕啦！"

"狗熊有啥怕的，以前又不是没出现过狗熊？！"

"这狗熊可是成了精了！上个月来了个打猎的，也是开着辆小车来的，遇着了狗熊，狗熊一巴掌把半个屁股挖去了，人昏迷不醒地抬了下来，醒来说狗熊会说人话哩！"

"人会学着野物的声叫，哪里会有野物学人的话？"

"人都能学着野物的声叫，野物又怎么不能说人的话？"

"他一定是没打败狗熊，脸面上不能下来，胡诓哩。"

"反正是风声传得紧，来打猎的人少了。"

"那你就看着我怎么收拾这狗熊了！"

felt pleased with himself, reminded them that they needed to lift their feet a bit higher than usual because the roads in the mountains were uneven, then continued chatting with the fat woman: "Have there been many people coming to hunt recently?"

"Not so many. Didn't you hear that there's a black bear at the top of the mountain? They're all afraid!"

"What's frightening about a black bear? Haven't there been bears here before?"

"But this bear is a spirit! Last month there was a hunter, he was driving a small car, too, and he came across the bear. It tore off half of his backside with one swipe. The man passed out and had to be carried back down the mountain, and when he came to he said the bear could talk like a human!"

"People can learn animal calls, but how could a wild animal learn to speak?"

"If people can learn wild animal calls, why can't an animal learn to speak?"

"He couldn't kill the bear, so he made up a lie to save face."

"In any case, the rumor spread and now fewer people are coming to hunt."

"Well, you'll see how I take care of this black bear!"

　　夏清和胖子听到他们说狗熊，已围过来听，听得面色都苍白了，待到戚子绍说他能收拾狗熊，就问："你打过狗熊?"戚子绍说："当然打过狗熊的，不管是什么厉害的野物，你只要摸清它的习性，没有猎不了的。狗熊嘛，也是个笨，它只会直线扑，你就只拐着弯儿和它斗。如果你碰到了一群狗熊，那你就更好打了，你只需藏在一个地方向它们开枪，一枪或许撂倒一只，另一只便顺着子弹也冲过来，你姿势不动地一个一个打。再如果你能引诱着一只向你扑来，一闪身让它扑下崖畔，后边的也就一条线地扑下崖畔，你可以直接到崖畔下收获罢了!"两个女人眼里闪动了惊异的光，说道："这太精彩，太有刺激了，咱们不打那些崖鸡子了，一定要到山顶去猎狗熊!"

　　王老板一直在用油布擦拭着车身，他不愿意把车继续往山顶的路上开。

Xia Qing and Chubby had heard them talking about the bear and came over to listen, their faces growing pale. When Qi Zishao said he was going to take care of it, they asked him, "Have you hunted bears before?" Qi Zishao said that of course he had hunted for bears. No matter how ferocious a wild animal was, you could hunt it if you knew its habits and behavior. A black bear was clumsy and only able to lunge in a straight line, so all you had to do was change directions and attack it. What if you came across a group of bears? Then you could hunt them even easier. All you had to do was hide somewhere and shoot in their direction. With one shot you might kill one, then another would rush at you following the report, and you could shoot them one after another without shifting your position. And finally, if you could lure one to rush toward you and then step out of the way so it lunged off a cliff, the bears behind it would leap off the cliff one after another and you could climb down to reap the game! The women's eyes flashed with amazement. "Wonderful, it's too exciting! Let's not hunt for those mountain pheasants, we have to go to the top of the mountain for the black bear!"

Mr. Wang had been wiping the body of the jeep with an oil rag. He didn't want to keep driving all the way to the top of the mountain.

"怎么能不去呢？"戚子绍说，"咱们不是打过熊吗？"

王老板含糊地点着头，说要去的话只能是他和戚子绍去，两个女人就留在这儿，这儿有吃有住的，又好玩，若去山顶遇见狗熊了，是该打狗熊呀还是顾及她们呀？

"咱是老猎手，还保护不了两个女人吗？"

两个女人欢喜跳跃，说："要去嘛，我们一定要去嘛！"

车重新发动起来，向深山钻去。两个小时后，路拐着"之"字形向秦岭的主峰爬。两边都是大的松树，路面上不时地出现了松鼠，但都是影子般地穿过公路。两个女人又是大呼小叫，要汽车能停下来，王老板没有听使唤，用力扳动着方向盘，因为弯道很大而路面又窄。突然间汽车油门加大，人似乎都飘起来，车的前面一只野兔在拼命地跑，"嘎"的一声刹住了，戚子绍首先下去，从路上捡起了一条兔子的尾巴，兔子则泥浆般贴在地上。

"We have to go," Qi Zishao said. "Haven't we hunted bears before?"

Mr. Wang nodded non-committedly and said that if Qi Zishao wanted to, then the two of them should go alone and leave the women here to amuse themselves where there were places to eat and sleep. If they went to the mountaintop and came across the bear, should they attack the bear or look after the women?

"We're experienced hunters, can't we protect two women?"

The women shrieked with excitement and said: "Let's go, we have to go!"

The jeep started off again, working its way deep into the mountains. Two hours later, the road zigzagged, climbing toward the highest peak in the Qin Mountains. Tall pines lined both sides of the road, and squirrels often appeared on the pavement, dashing across like shadows. The women were screaming and yelling again, wanting the jeep to stop, but Mr. Wang would not listen. He yanked the steering wheel around because the curves were sharp and the road narrow. Suddenly the throttle opened up and they seemed to be floating. In front of the jeep a hare ran for its life, and they screeched to a halt. Qi Zishao got out first and picked up the hare's tail from the road. The rest of the hare stuck to the ground like slurry.

到了道班，天就黄昏了。山顶道班是全程公路上最小的一个道班，只是一幢三间木屋，两个上了岁数的养路工。两个女人麻雀一般地喳喳乱叫，说这里是童话的世界，就在松树林子里捡蘑菇，采繁星般的小花。夏清说："我相信这里有各种各样动物的，动物都会说着人的话!"胖子噎道："你相信你也会长翅膀的!"两个女人闹起了小小的别扭。

可能是养路工寂寞得太久了，他们应允了客人就歇在这里，又提供吃的和喝的，但言语不多。尤其两个城市的女人向他们问这样那样的时候，显得手脚无措。木屋分两个小房间，原本两个养路工分住着，现在腾出一间来睡胖子和夏清，而在路的北边撑了军用帐篷，只有戚子绍和王老板去睡了。夏清对睡帐篷感兴趣，但帐篷里毕竟潮湿，保不住夜里又有什么野物闯进来。胖子便把木房里的旧的被褥抱出来，替换了带来的毛毯。"如果被褥上有虱子，"她说，"让吸有

They reached a highway maintenance station at dusk. This mountaintop depot was the smallest along the entire road, with only a three-room wooden cabin and a maintenance crew of two elderly men. The women chattered randomly like sparrows, saying that this was a fairy tale world where they would gather mushrooms in the pine forest and pick the small flowers that looked like clusters of stars. Xia Qing said: "I believe all the different kinds of animals here can speak!" Chubby rounded on her: "Do you believe you can grow wings, too?" They had a minor falling out.

Maybe the road maintenance workers had been alone for too long. They agreed to let the visitors stay and supplied things to eat and drink. They did not say much, and when the two city women asked them about this and that, they became awkward and clumsy. The cabin was divided into two small bedrooms, normally shared between the two road workers. They cleared a room for Chubby and Xia Qing and pitched an army tent on the north side of the road where Qi Zishao and Mr. Wang would sleep. Xia Qing showed an interest in sleeping in a tent, but after all the tent was damp inside and they could not guarantee what animals might force their way in during the night. Chubby gathered up all the old bedding in the cabin and brought it out to the tent, replacing it with the blankets they had brought with them. "If there are lice in the

钱有权人的血去!"

戚子绍换上了一身的猎装，在林子里踱过来踱过去，感觉非常地好。后来采着了一朵红色的七瓣花回到木屋，夏清已烧了一盆水洗脸洗手，戚子绍将花插在她头上了，说："让我也洗洗。"手伸进盆了，在水里抓住了一双嫩手。夏清往出抽，抽不动，拿眼睛看了一下帐篷边的胖子，不动了，手觉得越来越小。

"要是只来你一个人多好。"

"这不可能。"

"为什么？"

"第一次见你的时候，她并不想让我见你的，后来想了想，才领我上去……"

"你要是没上来，我也不用她的配件了。"

"……"

bedding," she said, "they can drink the blood of the rich and powerful!"

Qi Zishao changed into his hunting gear and paced back and forth in the woods for a while in a very good mood, then he picked a red flower with seven petals and returned to the cabin. Xia Qing had heated a pan of water to wash her face and hands. Qi Zishao stuck the flower in her hair and said: "Let me wash, too." His hands reached into the basin and seized the pair of delicate hands already in the water. Xia Qing tried to remove her hands, but couldn't extract them from his grip. She raised her eyes in the direction of Chubby over by the tent, and did not move. Her hands felt like they were growing smaller.

"It would have been so much better if you'd come by yourself."

"I couldn't."

"Why not?"

"The first time she met you, she didn't want to introduce me. Then later she decided to bring me along..."

" If you hadn't come, I wouldn't have used her accessories."

Xia Qing paused.

"她真会利用你!"

"她也保护我。"

"傻姑娘!"

"……她也漂亮哩。"

"是吗? 我没感觉。"

帐篷边胖子在嘎嘎地笑, 王老板在系帐篷门口的绳子时说了什么趣话, 胖子拿拳头捶王老板的背, 嚷叫: "你坏, 你坏!" 夏清再次要把手抽出来, 戚子绍低下头去, 迅速地吻了一下那根中指, 夏清就鹿一样地跑去了, 叫喊着: "打牌, 打牌呀!"

帐篷里的光线已经幽暗, 四个人并没有玩"升级", 戚子绍要教给大家一种扑克算命法。他光是默想了一个念头算了一次, 情绪颇高, 胖子问你算的是什么, 他笑而不答, 胖子说你不说我也知道, 是谋算着夏清吧。戚子绍说: "即便

"She's using you!"

"She also protects me."

"Stupid girl!"

"She's pretty, too."

"Is she? I hadn't noticed."

Outside by the tent Chubby was cackling at something amusing Mr. Wang had said as he tied the flap of the tent door with a rope. She pounded on his back with her fists, howling: "You're so bad! So bad!" Xia Qing tried once more to pull her hands out of the water. Qi Zishao lowered his head and swiftly kissed her middle finger. Xia Qing ran outside like a fleeing deer, shouting: "Let's play cards!"

Inside the tent it was already growing dark. Instead of playing a four-person game of Hundred, Qi Zishao wanted to teach everyone a way to tell fortunes with cards. He dealt the cards, silently contemplating a single thought, his emotions running high. Chubby asked, "Whose fortune are you planning to tell?" He smiled and would not answer. Chubby said, "Even if you won't say, I already know you're planning to tell Xia Qing's fortune." Qi Zishao said: "Since I love Xia Qing, that is my privilege, and there's nothing wrong with it!" Xia

爱夏清，那也是我的权利，这没什么错呀！"夏清已经脖脸通红，把扑克拨乱，说："都胡说，胡说！"戚子绍趁机张狂了，当场挑明他就爱上了夏清，爱上了夏清但能不能离掉现在的老婆，会不会最后娶了夏清，这得看天意了。就以某种牌代表能结婚，以某种牌代表不能结婚，重新洗牌起牌。大家都屏了气息看翻牌的结果，竟然是代表能结婚的牌首先被翻了出来。戚子绍就说："夏清，你也是亲眼看了，你要等着我！"夏清一时无语，眼睛扑忽扑忽地闪。胖子说："夏清真老实，你以为他说的真话？"戚子绍说："信不了我也该信牌呀！"王老板就让给他的房地产生意算一下，算出来的结果也是好的。王老板就说："既然做房地产能成功，你得支持我了。"戚子绍没有回应，却问："你觉得夏清怎么样？"王老板说："好嘛。"戚子绍问："怎么个好？"王老板说："五官好，身架子也好。"戚子绍说："夏清有综合之美！"胖

Qing's face and neck turned crimson. She scattered the cards and said: "Nonsense, you don't mean it!" Qi Zishao saw his chance, felt emboldened, and professed on the spot that he had fallen in love with Xia Qing. He was in love with Xia Qing, but whether or not he would leave his current wife, whether or not he would marry Xia Qing, depended on the will of fate. A certain card signified that they would marry, another card signified they would never marry. He shuffled the cards again and dealt them. Everyone held their breath to see the result, and the first card turned over was the card that meant they would marry. Qi Zishao said, "Xia Qing, you've seen it with your own eyes, you will have to wait for me." Xia Qing said nothing for a space, her eyes darting around and shining. Chubby said: "Xia Qing, you really are naive, do you think he's telling the truth?" Qi Zishao said: "Believe the cards if you don't believe me!" Mr. Wang wanted the fortune of his real estate business told, and the result was also favorable. Mr. Wang said: "Since my real estate business will succeed, you should back me." Qi Zishao didn't answer, asking instead: "What do you think of Xia Qing?" Mr. Wang said: "I like her." Qi Zishao asked: "What do you like about her?" Mr. Wang said: "Her features, and she carries herself well." Qi

子说:"呀呀,世上还有什么好词? 可别忘了,这么好的人是谁给你介绍的?"戚子绍说:"这一句话你说得好,得感谢你,晚饭咱要喝酒,炒熊掌吃!"

当戚子绍从帐篷里出来,似乎觉得夏清差不多已经是他的人,哼着小调往木屋去,一进门就喊:"晚饭吃什么呀?"

木屋里烟雾腾腾,锅灶边只看到养路工汗油闪亮的脑袋,他还把面条往开水锅里煮。

"没有炒熊掌吗?"戚子绍说。

"哪儿会有熊掌。"养路工说。

"别的野味呢,譬如黄羊、果子狸、崖鸡子?"

"用菌子做了汤。"

"只有菌子?"

这使戚子绍很丧气。

胖子说:"瞧,他的话落实不了吧?"拉了夏清到房间里

Zishao said: "Xia Qing is beautiful in every way!" Chubby said: "Well, are there any compliments left in the world? Don't forget who introduced you to such a nice woman." Qi Zishao said: "You're right, it's thanks to you. We should drink at dinner and eat bear paw!"

Qi Zishao emerged from the tent feeling as though Xia Qing was already his. He entered the cabin humming a little tune, then shouted as he walked through the door: "What are we eating for dinner?"

All he could see through the billowing clouds of steam inside the cabin was the head of one of the road workers glistening with sweat as he stood by the stove putting noodles into a pot of boiling water.

"Don't you have bear paw?" Qi Zishao asked.

"Who has bear paw?" the road worker said.

"Do you have any other wild game, like gazelle, masked civet, mountain pheasant?"

"Soup made with mushrooms."

"Only mushrooms?"

Qi Zishao was disappointed.

"See, can you be sure of what he says?" Chubby said as

去了。戚子绍听见夏清在房间里还说了一句："我就要吃熊掌嘛！"故意提高了声音和养路工说话："听说山上又有了狗熊啊？"

"是有吧。"养路工说。

"怎么不打了狗熊吃呢？"

"我们都在这山上。"

"你们？你是指你和狗熊吗？"

"是吧。"

戚子绍进了房间，说两个养路工是素食主义者，他们常年待在山上认那些野物都是同类了。"我现在明白了，"他说，"山下边嚷道狗熊成精了，会说人话，一定是他们传出来的，为的是不让别人捕猎。你们没注意他们的模样也差不多快要像狗熊了，腰粗屁股圆的，行动迟缓，还不停地吭哧吭哧着。"

she pulled Xia Qing into the bedroom. Qi Zishao heard one more thing Xia Qing said from the other room: "I want to eat bear paw!" He deliberately raised his voice and said to the road worker: "I hear there's a black bear up in the mountain."

"There is," the road worker answered.

"Why don't you kill the bear and eat it?"

"We both live on this mountain."

"Both? You mean you and the black bear?"

"Yes."

Qi Zishao went into the next room and told the others that the two road workers were vegetarians. After so many years living in the mountains they thought that wild animals were the same as humans. "Now I understand," he said, "All that panic at the foot of the mountain about a black bear who's a spirit, who can talk like a human, it must be a rumor they spread around because they don't want anyone to hunt it. Did you notice that they almost look like bears themselves, with their thick waists and round butts, the way they lumber and growl?"

He did not convince Xia Qing, who insisted: "I want you to get me bear paw!"

戚子绍说没有道理，夏清却仍在说："我偏要你给我熊掌吃！"

"我会的，小姐！"

"戚处长，这可是你说的，"胖子说，"吃不到熊掌我们就不走啦！"

吃过面条，两个女人就在房间的炕上歇下了，她们光着脚，披散了头发，脱去了外套而紧窄的内衣使身体该瘦的地方都瘦下去，该胖的地方都胖起来。戚子绍和王老板在房里赞美了一通女人形体的艺术，对面房间里的养路工就起了鼾声，屋外十分地安静，偶尔有车辆呼啸地从公路上驶下山去，听到的就是松塔落地的声音。说好的今晚上都不要睡，直聊到天亮，两个女人却很快就显出倦容。慵懒的姿态是特别惹人爱怜的，戚子绍满嘴的口水，言语开始放荡，王老板就说他是困了，打了哈欠去了帐篷。王老板一走，两个女人

"Miss, I will do it for you!"

"Director Qi, you said it yourself," Chubby said, "If we don't get to eat bear paw, we won't leave!"

After they ate their meal of noodles, the women went to rest on the heated brick bed platform called a *kang*. They were barefoot, and, letting their hair hang loose, they removed their outer clothing so that their tight underclothes showed their bodies to be thin and plump in the right places. Qi Zishao and Mr. Wang stayed in the room with them praising the art of the female form, while in the other room the road workers began to snore, and outside it was so extremely still that, except for the occasional car whizzing past along the road down the mountain, they could hear the sound of pinecones dropping. They had all decided together that they would stay up talking until daybreak instead of going to bed, but the women soon began to act sleepy. Their languid attitude invited tender thoughts, and Qi Zishao's mouth filled with saliva as his speech grew freer. Mr. Wang said he was tired, yawned, and went out to his tent. Once Mr. Wang left, the women leant back side-by-side against the head of the *kang* and chatted with Qi Zishao. The more they talked the further their bodies slid

就并排靠在炕头上和戚子绍说话，越说身子越往下溜，后来就躺下去，而且胖子的眼睛也合上了。戚子绍真想胖子是睡着了，他就敢去和夏清接近一番，但胖子偏是躺在炕的边上，让夏清躺在靠墙的里边，又不知道胖子是真的睡着了还是假睡，他不敢造次。

"养路工在山上待久了，真的能和野物和平共处吗?"夏清说，"那么，山上所有的野物都能认识他们了?"

"动物都是有灵性的。"

屋外有什么鸟在叫，一声长一声短，长长短短的。

"听见了吗，鸟在说话了!"

"你能听懂它们的话?"

"我是猎人呀!"

"这鸟在说什么?"

"一个说：你在哪儿? 一个说：在你心里。一个说：干

down the bed until at last they were reclining, and Chubby shut her eyes. If Qi Zishao had been certain Chubby was asleep, he might have dared to approach Xia Qing. Chubby was lying on the outside of the *kang* so that Xia Qing had to lie on the inside against the wall. Without knowing whether Chubby was really asleep or just pretending, he couldn't be indiscreet.

"When the road workers stay in the mountains for so long, can they really live in harmony with the wild animals?" Xia Qing asked. "Do all the animals on the mountain know them?"

"All animals have intelligence."

Outside a bird called, one long cry and one short, long and then short again.

"Did you hear? The birds are talking!"

"Do you understand what they're saying?"

"I am a hunter!"

"What are the birds saying?"

"One said: Where are you? The other said: In your heart. One said: What are you doing? The other said: Thinking of you!"

啥哩？一个说：想你哩！"

夏清挤了一下眉眼，她知道戚子绍在给她骚情。戚子绍却走过来，一下子捏住了她伸在炕边的脚。她吓了一跳，用手指指胖子。胖子睁开眼来，说："你去睡吧，我可困得不行了！"

"那你怎么就不睡着呢?!"

戚子绍说了一句，离开了房间，胖子猴一样跳下炕就把房间门关了。戚子绍听见了快速的关门声，心里有些不悦，站在门外了发现山顶上的夜黑，黑得伸手不见五指。这时候，公路上有一辆车驶过，他往路边闪了闪，但车依然挂了他的衣服就跌倒了。车剧烈地刹住，司机从车窗探出头来，看见他已经爬了起来，问：没事吧？戚子绍勃然大怒："你是怎么开车的？你要把我轧死了，我再和你小子说！"但车却"呼"的一声开走了。

Xia Qing narrowed her eyes, she knew Qi Zishao was playing on her feelings. Qi Zishao stepped over abruptly and squeezed her foot stretched out on the *kang*. Xia Qing was taken aback and pointed at Chubby. Chubby opened her eyes and said: "Go to sleep, I'm exhausted!"

"Then why aren't you asleep?"

Qi Zishao left the cabin, and Chubby hopped down from the *kang* like a monkey to close the door. He heard the sound of the door hastily shutting. Standing unhappily outside he discovered how dark the night was this high up in the mountains, so black he could not see the fingers of his outstretched hand. A car drove past and he stepped to the side of the road but it snagged his clothing, knocking him down. The driver slammed on the brakes and stuck his head out of the window, saw that Qi Zishao was already scrambling to his feet, and asked, "Are you alright?" Qi Zishao was furious: "You think you know how to drive? If you'd run me over, I'd have it out with you, you idiot!" The engine revved suddenly and the car drove away.

Mr. Wang heard the noise and emerged from his tent to make sure everything was alright. He said: "If he had run you

王老板闻声从帐篷里出来，瞧着真的没事，就说："真把你轧死了你怎么和人家说?!"戚子绍气咻咻又骂了一句，自己也笑了。

第二天早上，四个人又坐在车里往山上行驶了一段路，戚子绍和王老板就拿了枪往树林子深处走。胖子和夏清不愿意留在车里，也要厮跟着，和王老板吵了一架，戚子绍没了办法，就叮咛王老板要寸步不离她们。他们走过了一面斜坡，草丛里就发现了熊粪，胖子不相信是熊的粪，戚子绍便用树棍拨着粪讲解。扭头见王老板和夏清还在后边，就趁势抱了一下胖子的腰。胖子说："你不爱我，你爱夏清的。"戚子绍说："也爱的。"胖子说："我这腰粗，你抱不住的。"戚子绍用力抱了一下，放下了，说："你要不是我乡党的老婆我肯定就把你……"戚子绍知道自己在应付，但胖子也是女人，需要安慰的，果然瞧见胖子高兴了，在说："我其实不

over, how could you have it out with anyone?" Qi Zishao cursed some more, panting, then began to laugh himself.

The next morning the four of them got back into the jeep and drove further up the mountain. Qi Zishao and Mr. Wang picked up their rifles and walked into the forest. Chubby and Xia Qing didn't want to stay behind in the jeep and asked to go along, starting a quarrel with Mr. Wang. Qi Zishao could not do anything with the women, so he warned Mr. Wang not to step away from them even for a moment. They walked up the slope and discovered bear droppings in a clump of grass. Chubby would not believe it was really bear shit. Qi Zishao poked the droppings with a branch and explained, turning around to check that Mr. Wang and Xia Qing were still behind them, then took his chances at embracing Chubby around the waist. Chubby said: "You don't love me, you love Xia Qing." Qi Zishao said: "I love you, too." Chubby said: "My waist is so big you can't get your arms around it." Qi Zishao wrapped his arms around her and squeezed before letting go: "If you weren't married to someone I know, I would take you and..." Qi Zishao knew he was settling, but Chubby was a woman, too, and needed encouragement. Chubby was clearly pleased,

是胖，是丰满哩。"

夏清去了坡下的崖坎后小解，三个人坐在坡上等了一会儿，夏清还是没有上来，却有了一声尖叫。戚子绍立即让王老板拉了胖子往坡上去，自个就跑下崖坎。原来是夏清也发现一堆熊粪，而且熊粪是湿的。戚子绍就又喊王老板快把两个女人送回到车上，不管发生了什么事情都不要开车门下来。夏清才一走，他就提枪继续往坡上走，走了一里，果然就看见了一只狗熊，狗熊正蜷成一团在蒿草丛里睡觉哩。

"叭！"戚子绍瞄准着放了一枪。

狗熊翻了一个滚儿，滚出了草丛，窝在一块长满了苔藓的石头后。

戚子绍兴奋地跑过去，他没有想到今天打猎是这么顺当和容易，在他动手去提狗熊的后腿要把它翻过来的时候，他想到这只狗熊的掌真大，是让养路工来烹饪呢还是拿到山下

she was saying: "I'm not fat, I'm just full-figured."

Xia Qing had gone down the slope to pee behind a ridge. The other three sat on the mountainside and waited a while. Before she had come back they heard a scream. Qi Zishao sent Mr. Wang to haul Chubby back up the slope and ran down the ridge. It turned out Xia Qing had discovered bear droppings, too, and they were still moist. Qi Zishao shouted at Mr. Wang to take the women back to the jeep. No matter what happened they should not open the doors or get out. When Xia Qing finally relented, Qi Zishao grabbed his rifle and turned back up the ridge. He walked about half a kilometer before spotting a black bear curled up asleep in a thick growth of wormwood.

Crack! Qi Zishao took aim and fired.

The black bear tumbled out of the grass and rolled behind a moss-covered rock.

Qi Zishao ran over excitedly. He could hardly believe the day's hunting had gone so smoothly. As he reached out to lift the bear's hind leg to turn it over, he was thinking of how large the bear's paws were and whether he should let the road maintenance crew cook them or bring them to the little restaurant at the bottom of the mountain to be stir-fried. "No,

那个小饭馆去爆炒？"不，养路工是反对吃荤的，"他自言自语道，"让肥胖女人做，要做得没一点腥味。"但是，戚子绍刚刚提住狗熊的后腿，狗熊却忽地站了起来，黑乎乎的一座小山一样，他被压住了，那只熊掌就踩在他的胸口，他有些喘不过气来。

"你想死还是想活？"

戚子绍听见了一句人声，扭头看看周围，周围并没有人，声音是从狗熊的口里发出的。狗熊真的会说人话呀，戚子绍眼前一阵漆黑，他知道他是遇见了那只传说中的成了精的狗熊。

"想活。"他说，他还能说什么呢？

"想活？那让我把你干一下。"

戚子绍脑子里还没有转过弯来，他已经被狗熊提起来翻了个身，而且裤子就被抓了下来。他感到了屁眼非常地痛。

the road workers don't believe in eating meat," he said to himself, "The fat woman can cook them so they don't taste gamy." But just as Qi Zishao lifted the bear's hind leg, the bear suddenly stood, looming over him like a black hill. He was crushed to the ground, the bear's paw pressing on his breastbone so that he struggled to breathe.

"Do you want to live or die?"

Qi Zishao heard a human voice. He twisted his neck to look around, but no one was there. The voice was coming from the bear's mouth. It really could speak like a human. Everything went dark before Qi Zishao's eyes, and he knew he had encountered the legendary bear spirit.

"I want to live," he said. What else could he say?

"You want to live? Then let me abuse you."

Before Qi Zishao's mind could process what was happening, the black bear had already lifted him up, turned him over, and yanked down his trousers. He felt an intense pain in his anus. Afterward, he watched helplessly as the bear lumbered into the distance following a line of white birches.

Qi Zishao dragged himself back, his clothing filthy, his rumps thrust backward, limping with each step. The others

然后，眼看着狗熊顺着一行白桦树一步步走远了。

戚子绍狼狈地返回来，他的衣衫肮脏不堪，屁股撅着，一跛一跛的。大家忙问怎么着，是碰着狗熊了吗？戚子绍说他和狗熊突然遭遇了，他打了一枪，把狗熊的前腿打折了，他去追时狗熊却一抱头从荆棘丛里往沟下滚，他也滚，滚在半坡被树杈挡住了，只好回来。

他们回到道班的木屋里吃饭。王老板和两个女人为戚子绍敬酒，虽然没有猎到狗熊，但他们已为他的不凡的身手而佩服了，戚子绍是喝了很多酒，心里郁闷，脑袋就晕晕乎乎，说要睡觉就睡下了。一觉醒来，又是个黄昏，但这个黄昏比不得昨天的黄昏，月亮早早地就挂在西边山峰上。戚子绍听见王老板和两个女人在房间的土炕上打扑克，他就提了枪往山上去了。

越往山上去，越是风清月明，露水已经潮上来，渐渐湿

rushed to ask him what had happened. Had he found the black bear? Qi Zishao said he had come upon the black bear suddenly and fired his rifle, shattering the bear's forepaw, but when he went to chase it, the bear covered its head and tumbled through the brambles down into a gully. Qi Zishao tumbled after it, rolling halfway down the slope where he got caught in the undergrowth and had to turn back.

They returned to the highway maintenance station and ate a meal at the cabin. Mr. Wang and the two women raised toasts to Qi Zishao in recognition of his uncommon skill, even though he hadn't bagged the bear. Qi Zishao drank a great deal, his heart full of gloom and his head spinning. He said he needed to sleep and went to bed. When he woke it was dusk again, but this evening was nothing like the dark night before. The moon rose early and hung on the peak of the mountain to the west. Qi Zishao heard Mr. Wang and the women inside the cabin playing cards on the brick *kang*. He grabbed his rifle and headed back up the mountain.

The further he went up the mountain, the lovelier the night became with gentle breezes and a clear moon. Dew was already collecting, and it gradually dampened the legs of his

了裤腿，戚子绍在林子里的一块草坪上长长吁了一口闷气，看见了狗熊在一口山泉边喝水，忙呸了一口，呸出了半截咬断的牙齿，同时开了一枪。狗熊在枪响中一只脚栽倒在了泉里，接着脑袋也栽倒在了泉里，不一会儿整个熊都栽倒在了泉里，水哗啦地扑溅出泉沿。戚子绍跑近去，才要想着怎样才能把死了的狗熊从泉里弄出来，狗熊忽地又从泉里腾跃而起将他压在熊掌下了。

"你是想死还是想活？"狗熊又在说人话。

"想活。"他说。

"那让我再把你干一次。"

戚子绍自个翻了个身，把裤子拉下来，他听见了水声，屁眼更是钻心地痛。

戚子绍是踉踉跄跄地赶回来，王老板和两个女人还在木屋土炕上打扑克。他们不知道戚子绍又出去打猎了，也没有

trousers. Qi Zishao heaved a long sigh in a grassy clearing, then saw the black bear drinking from a mountain spring. He spit out half of a broken tooth at the same moment he fired his rifle. As the shot rang out one of the bear's paws dropped into the stream, then its head fell forward into the water, and almost at once its entire body toppled into the stream, splashing water over the banks with a crash. Qi Zishao ran closer, now wondering how he would get the dead bear out of the spring, when it suddenly sprang back out of the water and pressed him to the ground under its paw.

"Do you want to live or die?" The bear spoke like a human again.

"I want to live," he said.

"Then let me abuse you again."

Qi Zishao turned over on his own and pulled down his trousers. He heard the sound of the water. The pain driving into his backside was even worse.

Qi Zishao staggered back to the cabin in a hurry. Mr. Wang and the women were still playing cards on the *kang*. They hadn't realized Qi Zishao had gone out hunting again or heard the rifle shot, so when he entered the cabin they had a

听到枪声，当戚子绍进了木屋，他们嘲笑着戚子绍一醉竟能

醉大半天，睡起来还是形容憔悴，衣衫不整！戚子绍只好笑

笑，说他也要打牌的。

"你走路怎么啦！"夏清说，"匡着腿？"

"上了火，痔疮犯了。"

"烂尻子！"

两个女人哈哈笑起来，她们开始用一种暗语对话，音调

极轻极快，戚子绍觉得是外语，听起来嗡嗡一团。

"请说汉语！"戚子绍有些难堪，他听不懂她们的对话，

但他猜想一定是在说着他的坏话了。

"我们说的是重叠音。"夏清说。

两个女人又对话了一番，戚子绍听出是把每个字音重复

一次，但因为说得轻而快，他只能听出前边一句，后边的又

不知说什么了，而夏清的脸顿时绯红。

good time making fun of him, saying once he got drunk he stayed drunk all day, and even after napping he looked haggard and his clothing was a mess! Qi Zishao forced a smile and said he wanted to play cards with them.

"Why are you walking like that?" Xia Qing said, "Like a bowlegged man."

"Internal heat, an attack of hemorrhoids."

"Rotten bum!"

The two women started to laugh and began speaking to each other in a kind of code, pitched extremely fast and quiet. Qi Zishao thought it was a foreign language. It sounded like a mass of buzzing to him.

"Please, speak in Chinese!" Qi Zishao found it intolerable. Even though he couldn't understand them, he guessed they were saying nasty things about him.

"We're speaking in doubled syllables," Xia Qing said.

The women continued speaking to each other in code. Qi Zishao could make out that every syllable was repeated once, but because they spoke softly and quickly he could only understand the first part of the sentence and not what followed. Xia Qing's face went instantly scarlet.

"你们再这样说话，我得抽你们舌头了!"

"他俩合伙欺负我!"夏清说。

"是王老板喜欢上你的搭档了?"

"是喜欢上了，戚处长，"胖子说，"但你一定不会吃醋的，因为我们决定要牺牲夏清了!"

说罢，王老板竟揽了胖子的腰走出了木屋。

"哎哎，"戚子绍故意地叫着，却把木屋的房间门掩了，笑笑说:"再不牺牲，贷款和推销的事恐怕就吹了。"回过头来，夏清却端端直直坐在炕上。戚子绍去摸了一下她的脚，她的脚缩了，又去拉她胳膊，她往炕角退，说:"他们要牺牲我，我却不愿意哩。你坐好，咱们说说话不行吗?"

但戚子绍一时没话可说。

"说狗熊的事吧。"夏清说。

"那就说狗熊吧，"戚子绍说，"狗熊是世上最丑的野物，

"If you keep talking like this, I'll pull out your tongues!"

"The two of them teamed up to bully me!" Xia Qing said.

"Mr. Wang took a fancy to your partner?"

"I did, Director Qi," Chubby said. "But you can't be jealous, because we've decided to sacrifice Xia Qing!"

After she said this, Mr. Wang put his arm around Chubby's waist and they walked out of the cabin.

"Hey!" Qi Zishao shouted deliberately, although he shut the cabin door and laughed: "Their credit loans and sales promotion would be over unless they sacrificed you." He turned around, Xia Qing sat bolt upright on the *kang*. Qi Zishao stroked her foot, which shrank back, then he went to tug her arm, and she retreated to the corner of the bed, saying: "They want to sacrifice me, but I don't want to be sacrificed. Why don't you sit down, and we can talk for a while?"

Qi Zishao had nothing to say at the moment.

"We could talk about the bear," Xia Qing said.

"Let's talk about the bear then," Qi Zishao said. "Bears are the ugliest animals in the world, and also the worst of the

也是最坏的野物，我和它不共戴天，我一定要把它打死，我一定能把它打死！"

"戚处长，你怎么啦？"

"你应该叫我戚哥！"

"戚哥，你怎么突然恨起狗熊啦？"

戚子绍"哦"了一声，恢复了平和，说："我是有过猎狗熊的经历的。那一年我们猎狗熊，我是没经验的，放了一枪，它竟顺着枪子朝我扑来。狗熊的掌只要抓一下你，就会抓下你一个膀子的。旁边人就喊快趴下装死！我告诉你，狗熊是不吃尸体的，但它不知道人会装死。我就趴下装死了。狗熊过来拨我的腿，我不动。狗熊又过来拨我的头，我还是不动。狗熊就把鼻子凑近我的鼻子试，还有没有气儿，我闭住了气，仍是不动。我是猎人，我斗不过狗熊吗？！狗熊真以为我就是尸体了，就坐在那里发呆。我开始摸枪，拉动了

wild animals. The bear is my mortal enemy, we can't live in the same world. I will kill it, I have to kill it!"

"Director Qi, what's wrong with you?"

"You should call me Brother Qi!"

"Brother Qi, why do you hate bears all of a sudden?"

"Oh..." said Qi Zishao, and recovered his composure: "I've hunted bears before. The first time I hunted for black bear, I was inexperienced. I fired my rifle and the bear lunged toward me, following the report of the gun. A bear can rip off one of your arms with a swipe of its paw. The man next to me shouted, "Lie flat on the ground and pretend to be dead." You see, a bear won't eat a carcass, and it doesn't know that humans can pretend to be dead. So I dropped to the ground and played dead. The bear came over and poked my leg, but I didn't move. Then the bear prodded my head, but I wouldn't move. The bear put his snout next to my nose to test whether I was still breathing, so I held my breath and still didn't move. I am a hunter. Can't I outwit a bear? The bear believed that I was a corpse and just sat there. I began to feel for my rifle to pull the bolt. I knew it would make a noise and I would have to

枪栓，但拉动枪栓要出响声的，我必须在它扭头过来的瞬间一枪打死它，要不然狗熊即使不挖我，它一屁股坐我身上我也会被压死的。狗熊果然扭过了头，瞧我还活着，就张开了嘴要来咬我，我的枪响了，这一枪就打进它的嘴里，把它打死了。你不信？你到我家去，我家地上铺着一张熊皮，那就是我打死的狗熊的皮。"

"我信的，戚哥！"夏清说。

"好了，我可以把那张熊皮送你了！"

夏清简直视戚子绍是英雄了，她的身子放松开来，一双脚从屁股下伸开来，直直地在炕上。戚子绍口里又汪出了水，但他的手没有敢过去。"我真的送给你！"他再一次说。

突然有了一声奇怪的嚎叫，寂静的夜里十分响亮，似乎山林里有了回音，加长了音节和嗡声，传递着一种神秘的恐惧。两个人立即停止了说话，戚子绍侧耳又听了一下，叫道："狗熊来了！"脸色寡白，随之通红，像喝过了酒，一下

kill the bear the second its head turned. The bear could crush me to death just by sitting on me, even if it didn't rip me apart. The bear turned its head, saw I was still alive, and opened its jaws to bite me. My gun went off, the bullet went into its mouth and killed it. You don't believe me? You should come to my house, there's a bearskin spread out on the floor. That's the skin of the bear I killed."

"I believe you, Brother Qi!" Xia Qing said.

"Alright, I will give you the bearskin!"

Xia Qing clearly regarded Qi Zishao as a hero. Her body relaxed and she unfolded her legs from underneath her buttocks, stretching them out on the *kang*. Saliva pooled in Qi Zishao's mouth, but he did not dare reach for her. "I really will give it to you!" he said again.

Suddenly they heard a strange howl, which reverberated in the stillness of the night. There seemed to be an echo in the mountain forest, an elongated syllable and booming sound that transmitted a mysterious dread. They stopped talking as Qi Zishao tilted his head to listen, then shouted: "The black bear is here!" His face blanched, then turned crimson as if he had

The Hunter
猎
人

子跳起来就要往外走。夏清也跳下炕，炕下边却一时寻不着鞋，而在帐篷里的王老板和胖子已经跑了过来，他们拿了枪，惊慌地说狗熊就在附近。

"来了好！"戚子绍极快地把子弹装上膛，说："我须报仇不可，这回我再不打死它，我就再不来打猎了！"从屋里跑了出去。

两个女人也要去，王老板这回发怒了，哐当把门拉闭，又在门闩上插上了木棍儿，提枪去撵戚子绍。夏清隔着门缝喊："我真的要吃上熊掌了！"

戚子绍是听到了夏清的喊声，他朝林子的深处跑，他的屁股还火烧火燎地痛，仍疯了一般地跑。山坡上没有狗熊，草坪上也没有狗熊。戚子绍又跑到山泉边，狗熊还是没有。王老板是一直追着他的，但王老板没能追上，他自叹不如，就坐下来等待枪响而辨别戚子绍的方位。

been drinking. He leapt up and moved toward the door. Xia Qing jumped down from the *kang* but could not find her shoes right away. Meanwhile Mr. Wang and Chubby had rushed out of the tent, both holding rifles, and were saying with alarm that the bear was nearby.

"Good!" Qi Zishao quickly loaded bullets into his rifle with a clang. "I must have revenge. If I don't kill it this time, I will never hunt again!" He ran from the room.

The two women wanted to go with him, but this time Mr. Wang was infuriated and slammed the door shut on them, sticking a piece of wood through the bolt before raising his rifle and running after Qi Zishao. Xia Qing shouted through the crack in the door: "I want to eat bear paw!"

Qi Zishao heard Xia Qing's shout, and he ran deeper into the forest. His backside still burned with pain, but he ran in a frenzy. The black bear was not on the mountainside. It was not in the grassy clearing. Qi Zishao ran back to the bank of the mountain stream. The bear was not there either. Mr. Wang was following the whole way, but could not catch up to him. He gave up the chase and sat down to wait for the sound of gunshots to reveal Qi Zishao's location.

戚子绍像一只没头的苍蝇，四处乱撞，越是寻不着狗熊越是复仇的火焰熊熊，又翻过一个崖嘴，终于发现了一个黑影在前边移动，他知道那是狗熊了。但这一次的戚子绍发誓要打死狗熊，又汲取了前两次的教训，他爬上了崖嘴。在崖嘴，他瞧见了月光下的一块平台石上，狗熊在那里蹭身子，就静静地瞄准着放了一枪。

"叭！"

这一枪是百分之百地打中了，狗熊是从平台石上跌了下去。戚子绍并没有立即下了崖嘴，他又瞄准了跌下去的狗熊放了一枪，狗熊就动也不动了。

"我要打烂你的×！"戚子绍骂着从崖嘴下去，站在了狗熊的面前，狗熊是四脚朝天地躺着，他踢了一下，已经不会动了，他端起了枪瞄准狗熊后腿中间的部位准备打三枪，不，打四枪，打它个稀巴烂！

Qi Zishao plunged wildly in every direction like a fly without a head. The longer he searched for the black bear, the hotter the flame of vengeance blazed in him. He reached an overhang in the cliff and finally discovered a shifting black shadow in front of him. He knew it was the black bear. He had sworn he would kill it, and this time, utilizing the lessons of his two previous encounters, he climbed up the overhang. From its edge he saw a flat stone formation in the moonlight and the black bear rubbing its body against the stone. He quietly took aim and fired.

"Crack!"

This bullet was a hundred percent on the mark. The black bear fell from the flat stone. Qi Zishao didn't come down from the edge of the cliff right away. Instead he took aim at the fallen bear and fired again. The bear stopped moving.

"I'll smash your ＊＊＊＊ to pieces!" Cursing, Qi Zishao walked down the ridge and stood in front of the bear, which lay there with all four legs pointing to the sky. He kicked the bear, and the bear did not move. He leveled his rifle and took aim between the bear's hind legs intending to fire three shots,

但是，这一次仍和上两次的情况一样，当戚子绍刚刚把四颗子弹装进了膛，狗熊却一下子扑上来抱了他在地上了，这次狗熊不是一只掌压着他，而是两只掌压着了他。

"你是想死还是想活？"

戚子绍是彻底地绝望了。他想起了夏清，不能给她吃熊掌，也不能送给她一张熊皮了。狗熊张合着满是牙齿的大嘴，锋利的掌爪搭在他的脖颈，月亮下他瞧见爪甲闪闪发着白光，戚子绍没有再说"想活"，其实他哪里不想能活下去，也没有主动去拉脱裤子，他知道狗熊即使不侮辱他，狗熊也不会再让他活着离开了。

"随便吧，"他说，"要干要吃你随便吧，我只是想问你一句：你到底是狗熊还是魔鬼，这么厉害?!"

"你问我？"狗熊说，"我正想问你呢，你到底是猎人还是卖屁股的?!"

no, four shots, and smash it to a pulp!

But this time was the same as the last two, and when Qi Zishao had loaded four bullets into his rifle, the black bear leapt up and crushed him to the ground. Now the bear held him down with two paws instead of one.

"Do you want to live or die?"

Qi Zishao gave up hope entirely. He thought of Xia Qing. He would not be able to feed her bear paw or give her a bearskin. The bear was opening and closing its large toothy jaws, its paws hanging over Qi Zishao's neck, and in the moonlight he could see the white gleam of its claws. Qi Zishao did not say "I want to live" again, believing he had no chance of living. He did not pull down his pants, knowing that even if the black bear did not humiliate him, it would not let him leave alive.

"Alright," he said, "You can eat me or abuse me. I just want to ask you a question first: you're so ferocious, are you really a bear or are you a demon-spirit?"

"Me?" the bear said. "I was going to ask you: are you a hunter or are you a man-whore?"

这个时候，趴在木屋窗口上的胖子和夏清听见了连续的两声枪响，欢叫如雀，急切地盼望戚子绍回来，她们可以吃到稀罕的熊掌了。

2002 年

At this moment Chubby and Xia Qing, who were leaning against the window of the cabin, heard two successive gunshots. They made joyful cries like sparrows, expectantly waiting for Qi Zishao to come back so they could eat the delicacy of the bear paw.

2002

附 录

Appendices

文学天空中的恒星

杨乐生

中国当代文学的发展变化中贾平凹始终是一个无法回避的存在。

三十多年以来，贾平凹在创作的诸多领域做出了骄人的成绩，用千余万言的百十本作品集，远远地走在了同时代人的前列，被目为中国文坛的奇迹。小说、散文、诗歌、文

A Fixed Star in the Literary Firmament

By Yang Lesheng

Translated by Denis Mair

In the development of contemporary literature, Jia Pingwa has been a constant presence that cannot be ignored.

Over the past thirty years, Jia's performance in various creative domains has been worth taking pride in. In one-hundred-odd works running to over ten million published characters, he has moved into the foremost rank of his contemporaries and won recognition as a miracle on the Chinese literary scene. Proceeding along the multiple tracks of fiction,

论、书法、绘画等多种艺术形式，齐头并进，全面开花，硕果累累。在华人写作圈中，洵为仅见。人们一方面钦佩他罕见的创造力，另一方面对他构筑的艺术世界更是感到吃惊。一个"农民"，一个孱弱的人，一个貌不惊人的人，一个嘴笨木讷的人，硬是在不可能处创造出了文学的奇迹！这不能不让我们叹为观止。一般而言，一个作家能在某一类体裁登峰造极已经很难得了，但贾平凹是在多个领域出类拔萃，领袖群伦。我们除了给他一句"天才式的作家"的结论外，恐怕很难再找出另外的高度来概括且做比较客观的评价。即以散文论，当代的散文家可谓多矣，但倘以贾平凹的散文成就为标准来衡量，我们又能列出几个当代中国的散文家呢？长篇小说的写作亦是同样的情形：贾平凹先后获得美国的"美孚飞马奖"（《浮躁》）、法国的"费米娜文学奖"（《废都》）、香港的"红楼梦文学奖"（《秦腔》）及中国的"茅盾文学奖"

essays, poetry, criticism, calligraphy and ink painting, he has flowered and borne fruit in each genre. Such a phenomenon is rarely seen within the circle of Sinophone writers. People are on one hand impressed by his creativity and on the other hand are amazed at the artistic world he has constructed. Here we have a "peasant," a weak physical specimen of unremarkable physiognomy, a halting speaker, but somehow he has presented us with an ongoing literary miracle. What are we to do but exclaim at the marvel of it?! In general, for a writer to attain the apex in one genre is hard enough, but Jia Pingwa stands at the apex in many areas. Aside from concluding that he is a literary genius, we would be hard put to find a superlative that could encapsulate and assess his value. Take his essays for example. There are plenty of contemporary essayists, but if we rate them by the standard set by Jia, not many of them will measure up. The situation is similar with respect to novel-writing. These are some of the prizes Jia has won for his novels: America's Pegasus Prize for Literature (*On Edge*), France's Prix Femina (*Ruined City*), Hong Kong's Dream of the Red Chamber Award (*Qin Opera*), and China's Mao Dun Literature Prize (*Qin Opera*). If we make a survey of

（《秦腔》）。放眼全中国的当代作家，大约尚未有第二人赢得这么多、这么高层次中外享有盛名的荣誉。他也是有大量作品被译介到国外为数并不多的当代作家中的一个。我们从这个侧面，就能观察到贾平凹的广泛影响。有人称贾平凹是"中国文坛的独行侠"，我看是见地之论，绝非溢美之词。

仅就中短篇小说的造诣而言，贾平凹就有着别人无法替代的独有价值，达到了崭新的艺术高度。这本书（《贾平凹作品精选》）的编选，首先要面对的是选择的艰难。贾平凹有大量的中短篇小说作品，已结集出版的有三十多种，字数在三百万字以上，如何取舍，是颇为为难的。在有限的篇幅中怎么做才能尽可能地显示出有贾平凹艺术特征的代表性的作品？是否要按他写作的先后时期分阶段选取？是以已经获奖的作品为主呢，还是以尽管存在争议但有着强烈的艺术探索精神的作品为主？是以专家学者已经达成共识的作品为主体还是

China's contemporary writers, it is not likely we will find another winner of so many top-level prizes both in China and abroad. He is one of the limited number of contemporaries whose writings are consistently translated for foreign publication. This gives us a sidelight on the breadth of Jia Pingwa's influence. It has been said that Jia is the "knight-errant"of Chinese literature. I consider this to be a trenchant assessment which is not at all effusive.

Let us speak specifically on Jia Pingwa's mastery of the short story form: he is irreplaceable due to the new artistic level to which he has taken this genre. Compilation of the present collection (*Selected Works of Jia Pingwa*), first of all, faces an embarrassment of riches. Jia has written numerous short stories and novellas which have been collected in over thirty published volumes, with a word count running to three million characters. Thus one hardly knows where to begin the selection process. In the space of a limited volume, how is one to choose stories that can represent Jia's unique traits as an artist? Should one choose by period of composition? Should one focus on prize-winning pieces? Should one choose pieces that are controversial due to their spirit of aesthetic exploration? Should one focus on critical consensus or on audience reception as a basis for selection? These are concrete

以各界读者的好评为标准？这些都是不可回避的具体问题，处理得不合适必然影响阅读效果。本书现在的做法是在征求了为数并不多的人的意见后，不面面俱到，不兼顾贾平凹的创作历程，不论题材，不分得奖与否的主次，不按发表顺序，只选作者艺术上成熟期的能充分体现作家个性的作品，向探索性的作品倾斜，侧重营造"商州"和指向现实的代表性作品。当然，如此一来肯定会漏掉大量的好作品，给人一种以偏概全之感，但愿这种"偏"能有独有的艺术含金量。

贾平凹对中国文坛最引人注目的贡献，是他用大量的作品在艺术上建构了一个"商州世界"。如果认为贾平凹热爱故乡并用手中的笔讴歌故乡，那么恐怕就小觑了贾平凹包容深广的艺术雄心，就忽略了贾平凹早已逸出地理上的商州的现代忧思和世界情怀。此商州非彼商州。贾平凹笔下的商州，其实就是艺术地认识中国的一个窗口，中国社会的一切

problems that cannot be evaded: if not handled fittingly, they will detract from the overall reading experience. The approach taken in the present collection was to solicit opinions, but only from a few advisers. No attempt was made to encompass all facets or include each creative stage; no consideration was given to subject matter; no priority was given to prize-winning pieces; and sequence of publication was not considered. Only works from his mature period were chosen, with preference given to exploratory pieces and with a secondary emphasis on typical evocations of Shangzhou and on his reality-oriented pieces. Of course, this approach is bound to omit many fine pieces and give an impression of partiality, but it is my wish that my "partiality" will hit upon a vein of high-grade artistic ore.

Jia Pingwa's most noteworthy contribution to the Chinese literary scene is his fashioning of the "world of Shangzhou" in a large number of works. If we suppose that these works are a paean to his home district, penned by its devoted son, that would be underestimating his far-reaching literary ambitions. It would also ignore his contemplative vision of modernity and his cosmopolitan outlook, which have long ago expanded beyond the geographical bounds of Shangzhou. His Shangzhou is not simply a district. As penned by Jia Pingwa, Shangzhou is really a window through which we can come to know China.

变化在这里都有着程度不同的反应，是透视中国的 X 光机。甚至可以反过来说，商州的律动就是中国的律动，商州的变化就是这个世界的变化。商州是贾平凹艺术的出发点，而其归宿点则是走出商州，走遍中国，走向世界。1990 年以前，贾平凹的中篇小说几乎全是写商州的，商州题材的短篇小说也为数不少。《天狗》《黑氏》《美穴地》等力作就是典型代表。这些作品或富含历史的厚重度，或包容现实的温热度，或曲尽人性的纵深度，从多个视角写活了生存在这片土地上的人和事。天狗、师娘、黑氏、柳子言等人物形象业已成为打下"贾氏印记"标志性的形象，其难得的艺术价值越来越得到广泛的认可。倘若再加上贾平凹写商州大量的散文和影响巨大的长篇小说，如《浮躁》《高老庄》及《秦腔》等，一个丰厚的、多彩的、立体的商州就屹立在人们面前了。当代中国作家中大概只有莫言的"高密东北乡"可以和贾平凹

All the transformations of Chinese society are reflected, more or less, in this body of work: it is an X-ray machine that shows us China from the inside. One could say that the pattern of events in Shangzhou is the pattern of events in China; the changes undergone by Shangzhou are those that the world undergoes. Shangzhou is the point of departure for Jia's art, but its direction goes beyond Shangzhou to cover the land mass of China and advances into the world at large. Almost all of Jia's novella's up to 1990 were about Shangzhou, and many of his short stories address the subject of Shangzhou. Classic examples of this are his masterworks—"Tiangou," "A Woman Named Black," and "Felicitous Site." These pieces in one respect are richly grounded in history; in another they embrace the here-and-now with warm regard, delving into deep-seated matters of human nature; from many angles they bring alive the people and events on this patch of land. Such personae as Tiangou, The Master's Wife, Woman-Named-Black and Liu Ziyan carry the iconic stamp of Jia's character portrayal, which has been winning increasingly wider acknowledgement from the public. Added to this are Jia's voluminous essays and his influential novels like *On Edge*, *Old Gao Village* and *Qin Opera* which present us with a rich, multi-hued-and-layered evocation of Shangzhou. Among contemporary Chinese writers, perhaps only Mo Yan's "Gaomi Township of Dongbei" can rival Jia's

Critique
评论

的"商州"相媲美。纵观中外文学，我们会发现一个相通的现象：不少杰出的作家都创造了一个自己的世界，而这个世界多和作家的故乡重叠。加西亚·马尔克斯的马孔多，威廉·福克纳的约克纳帕塔法，鲁迅的鲁镇和未庄，沈从文的湘西……这些艺术世界要比作家的故乡大得多，其作为一个文化符号已深深走进人们的心中。贾平凹的"商州"无疑是他创造的艺术世界，其所蕴藏的审美富矿今天尚未得到充分的开发，但可以预期，随着对贾平凹研究的深入，其特有的价值将会越来越显示出来。

长期以来，贾平凹致力于对中华传统艺术菁华的继承和发扬光大，几十年如一日未曾断绝，已经成功地创作出了一大批各类体裁的文学精品。从立意到结构，从语言到细节，从描写到叙述，无不在打通古今的意义上做出了成功的探索，是体现"中国形式"及"中国气魄"最具有代表性的作

imaginative construct. Taking an overview of Chinese and Western literature, we will find a shared phenomenon: Quite a few outstanding writers have created imaginary worlds of their own which are superimposed upon their home districts. For Gabriel García Márquezit it was Macondo; for William Faulkner it was Yoknapatawpha County; for Lu Xun it was Lu Town and Wei Village; for Shen Congwen it was West Hunan. These artistic worlds exceed the scope of each writer's native district *per se*, and they have found a place in readers' hearts as cultural symbols. Jia Pingwa's Shangzhou is undoubtedly an artfully created world, constituting a rich aesthetic vein with plenty of reserves yet to be unearthed. Nevertheless, we can say with assurance that as research on Jia goes deeper, the special value in his imaginative world will be brought increasingly to light.

Over several decades, Jia Pingwa has endeavored to inherit and advance the essence of China's traditional art, never ceasing for a day. He has succeeded in creating a corpus of masterworks in various genres. Whether in terms of conception or structure, of language or plotting, of description or narrative, all his works grow out of his successful exploratory integrations of the classical and the modern. Among Chinese writers he is a prime exemplar of "Chinese form" and Chinese

家之一，甚至可以径称为典范性的作家之一。白话文运动距今近百年了，现代汉语到了现在是不是已经取得长足的进步和发展，恐怕是每一位关心中国文学的人必须面对的大问题，因为这个问题解决不好，中国文学的现代化云云就基本上是一句空话。任谁都知道文学是语言的艺术，但如何从语言臻于艺术的境界，说起来容易，做起来难上加难。只要看一看二十世纪以来的中国文学中有多少位作家形成了自己的语言个性，就会明白此问题的严峻性和迫切性。多少让人们感到遗憾的是：大多数作家（即便是成名或著名作家）尚谈不到文学的个性，更没几个人可以做到让读者只看语言文字而不看作者姓名就可以判断得出这是某人的作品。从新文化运动开始，一直到目前为止，也不过是胡适、周氏兄弟、老舍、沈从文、汪曾祺、金庸、王小波、贾平凹等十来个作家能让我们眼前一亮罢了。但愿我这个看法不至于太过片面和

"soul-force." In fact, we can point to him as a defining writer of our milieu. Now that the Chinese "vernacular movement" is nearly in its one-hundredth year, those who feel concerned for Chinese literature must face a major problem: has the modern Sinitic language made adequate strides in its development? If a solution is not found to this problem, then all talk of Chinese literature's modernization is baseless. Everyone knows that literature is the art of language, but as for how to reach an artistic plane in language, to speak is much easier than to act. We need only look at how many or few writers in the 20th century have forged their own linguistic personality to realize the gravity and urgency of this problem. It is regrettable that in the case of most writers, even well-known ones, we can hardly speak of literary personality, let alone the distinctiveness that enables us to identify an unattributed piece of writing. From the "New Culture Movement" right up to the present day, there have only been ten-or-so figures whose writing makes our eyes light up in recognition, namely Hu Shi, the Zhou brothers (Zhou Zuoren and Zhou Shuren), Lao She, Shen Congwen, Wang Zengqi, Jin Yong, Wang Xiaobo, Jia Pingwa and a few others. I hope my view on this does not prove to be one-sided and prejudiced.

Our modern and contemporary fiction writers and essayists

偏颇。现当代的小说家和作家全方位地受到"欧化"和苏联的影响，尤其是语言几乎是欧美语言的"汉语版"，也有一种叫法是"翻译体"，与中国语言的特性距离很大，在承继中国古来语言神气方面尤其让人不能满意。不能说用古汉语写作就不能在当代存在，我在此主要强调的是现代汉语在文学写作中的运用和发展问题，我固执地以为文学语言绝对制约文学可能的发展高度，这不是一个标准化问题，而是一个诗化、审美化性质的问题。中华民族形式涉及的方面甚多，语言仅是其中比较重要者之一，像贾平凹写作中"文白夹杂"的尝试，不敢说全都是成功的，但其求索的精神和不断实践的劳绩，谁也是否认不了的。其他如对白描手法的天才借鉴，当是有目共睹的事实。贾平凹对六朝志怪小说、唐宋传奇及明清笔记小说的借鉴和超越，更是他小说诱人的魅力所在。《太白山记》一组二十篇，笔法既老到又随意，短小

have been pervasively influenced by "Europeanization" and Soviet-era literature. Their language, for the most part, can be called a Sinitic version of European and American language. This is sometimes called "translationese": it is a far cry from the inherent features of the Chinese language, and it has not inherited its soul-force in a satisfactory way. This is not to say that writing in old-style Chinese cannot exist in a contemporary context. What I am emphasizing here is the utilization and development of modern Sinitic in literary writing. I am convinced that language determines the height to which literature can develop. This is not an issue of standardization; it is a matter of poetic and aesthetic substance. As a people the Chinese have generated forms touching on many areas, and literary language is only one such form, albeit an important one. I do not presume to say that Jia's attempts at a "vernacular-classical hybrid" mode are uniformly successful, but no one can deny his exploratory spirit and consistently industrious efforts. Anyone with eyes to see will appreciate other aspects of his talent, such as the techniques of rough sketching in his writing. Another appealing feature of his fiction is the way he draws on and goes beyond the mythic-and-grotesque stories in the Northern and Southern Dynasties, romances of the Tang-and-Song era and literary sketches in the Ming-and-Qing era. *Record of Taibai* is a series of twenty

精悍，有"新志怪"的感觉，有现实生存的悲悯情怀，又有佛教观念、禅理禅趣渗透，奇异博杂中不乏现代理性的观照，批判思索中可以体味到作者的达观和温厚，读后使人耳目一新，精神为之一振。有人可能会以为贾平凹喜欢神神道道，故意玩神秘的一套，岂不知从《山海经》《搜神记》开始，奇思异想，自由无羁，魔幻般的人和事一直是中国小说不曾断绝的特征之一，神秘文化也是中国文化不可或缺的一个组成部分，生命中本来就有很多说不清的东西。完全可以说贾平凹通过他的有关题材的表现，未尝不是为当代小说的发展寻觅到了一条新路。至于这条路如何朝下走，那就得要积之时日了。

贾平凹在全力摸索和追求文学上的"中国化"的同时，时刻也没有忘记用现代意识在内里支撑他的中短篇小说。乍一看，贾平凹笔下写的都是农村和农民。这再正常不过了，

short stories: they are penned in an accomplished yet casual manner, short but incisive, giving one the sense of a new style of the "mythic-and-grotesque". There is an empathy toward the realities of existence, but at the same time there are Buddhist ideas, imbued with a zen-like sense of intuitive enlightenment. Amid the mélange of oddities, one also finds cogitation in a rationally modern vein. Amid critical trains of thought one can sense the writer's tolerance and tenderness. After going through these pieces, the reader feels refreshed and energized. Some may hold the opinion that Jia Pingwa likes to traffic in the supernatural and deliberately plays with a mystical bag of tricks. Aren't they aware that starting from *Classic of Mountains and Seas* and *In Search of the Marvelous*, unbridled imaginings and fantasy elements have long been a feature of Chinese fiction? Mysticism is an inalienable component of Chinese culture, for there are many things in life which are inherently hard to explain. We could plausibly say that in such subject matter, Jia has found a path of development for modern Chinese fiction. As for how to press forward on this path, only time will tell.

While exerting his full energy to pursue literary "Chineseness," Jia Pingwa never forgets to infuse his short fiction with modern awareness that supports it from within. At first glance, it would seem that Jia's writings all deal with

Critique
评论

因为中国有八九亿农民，整个地球的 40％ 的农民共同在中国生存着，一个当代作家关注农民是他的责任、义务和天职。有点和沈从文自称"乡下人"相类似，贾平凹称自己为"我是农民"（这四个字恰好是他的一本书的名字），此不仅表明他们二人对乡里人的厚爱，更是彰显着他们谦卑、低调的美德和极端素朴的心灵。农民题材不在乎写或不写，关键是如何写，用什么样的艺术观念去写的问题。贾平凹在一九八〇年前后已经着意于文学观念的更新，写出来了《沙地》《厦屋婆悼文》《二月杏》《好了歌》等小说，引起争议并走在了当时全国小说界的前沿。他在小说创作上明显受到了日本川端康成和拉美作家略萨、鲁尔弗的影响，特别是川端康成"日本化"的艺术追求，对贾平凹的影响巨大。《黑氏》《天狗》等一系列作品就是在现代意识观照下的代表，人物的多样性、复杂性及由此带来的对人性的深刻艺术开掘是贾平凹

rural villages and peasants. There is nothing strange about this, because China has eight-to-nine hundred million peasants, which means that 40% of the world's total number of farmers live in China. For a contemporary writer to concern himself with farmers is a rightful obligation and a heaven-given vocation. Like Shen Congwen, who called himself a "man of the countryside," Jia Pingwa once declared, "I am a peasant." These four words happen to be the title of one of his books. Such a moniker does not just represent his fondness for rural people, it is also a sign of his humility, his homespun traits and his unassuming outlook. The crux of rural subject matter does not lie in whether you write about peasants but how you write about them, and what artistic conceptions you employ in writing about them. Way back around 1980, Jia had already made up his mind to update his literary conceptions, and out of this came stories like "Sandy Ground," "Elegy for Old Lady Xia Wu," "February Almonds," and "The Won-Done Song." These stirred up controversy and moved toward the cutting edge of fiction at the time. In his fictional creation he was obviously influenced by Japan's Yasunari Kawabata and the Latin American writers Vargas Llosa and Juan Rulfo, especially Kawabata's artistic ideal and pursuit of "Japanization." His serial stories on Shangzhou such as "A Woman Named Black" and "Tiangou" are representative of the modern mentality of

这个时期最为显豁的特点。贾平凹的中短篇小说在一九九〇年以后就不宜简单地用一句诸如"现实主义"或其他什么术语来评价了，它不是单一的，更多的是杂色，是多样性，是丰富性，是中国文化精神与现代性相杂糅的新品格。贾平凹非常注意对域外现代艺术的观念、形式、技巧的吸纳和"拿来"，即使个别作品略显生硬也在所不惜（如《晚唱》《病人》），充分体现出了他在平时生活中胆小但在艺术创造中极其大胆、常有出人意料之举的个性。《烟》不是一般的心理小说，也不是"意识流"就可以概括的，我更看重其对佛教"轮回"观念在作品中的化用，更喜欢他如梦似幻、飞扬起来的生命际遇。而《听来的故事》写作于晚近，篇幅极小，形式别致，用三个小故事串起来。既很古老又极现代，土洋结合，视野广阔，直指人类生存的困境、窘境及荒诞和荒谬；既温情洋溢，又忧愤幽深；文字老到，叙述简洁。显然

his writing. The abundance and complexity of character types, with the concurrent delving into human nature are salient features of his writings from that period. As for his short fiction after 1990, it can no longer be subsumed under "naturalism" or any other simple term. Far from being monochrome, it is many-hued, many-sided and richly varied. It is a new entity compounded of China's cultural spirit blended with modernity. Jia Pingwa applied himself to absorbing and even "appropriating" modern artistic concepts, forms and techniques from other lands. Although such combinations may come off somewhat stiffly in certain pieces such as "Evening Song" and "Sufferer", they fully embody his personality, which is cautious in matters of everyday life yet bold and surprisingly innovative in his artistic creations. "Tobacco" is not an ordinary psychological story, and it cannot be summed up as "stream of consciousness." What I value is the way he utilizes the Buddhist idea of reincarnation in the story. More than that, I like the dreamlike, swirling succession of life encounters. As for "A Story Someone Told Me," one of his recent efforts, it is a short, exquisite piece in which three story arcs are braided together. It is ageless yet modern, combining the native and the cosmopolitan. Its broad vision points directly at the predicament of human existence and the absurd inanities people get mired in. It is tender-hearted yet aggrieved; the

是厚积薄发之作，非斫轮老手无以办此。对人的一切的关注，是小说历久弥新的大主题。现代意义上的人比传统的人的观念要进步得多，关注的层面要丰富得多。全面地挖掘人的一切是贾平凹孜孜以求的，从早期的王满堂到近来的韩起祥，在众多不同的层面叫我们认识和欣赏了人类无限广阔的精神世界。而中国人，中国的各类人，尤其是在社会底层生活的人，在贾平凹心目中永远是最重要的观察、关注和书写对象。经过几十年的摸爬滚打、曲折坎坷地走到了今天，贾平凹已经达到了不去人为地提纯和净化，注重心理和情绪，将自然主义、神秘主义与现实主义及现代主义几大块融合在自己小说中的空前的艺术境界，成为一座中国当代文学中绕不过去的大山。

我们应该将作家贾平凹和作为艺术家的贾平凹结合起来考察，本文仅从中短篇小说中的角度做了一点粗浅讨论，肯

writing shows practiced ease; the narrative is spare. This is clearly a work that was long-incubated yet spontaneously released: it could only have been written by a consummate craftsman. A concern for all that is human has long been the overarching theme of fiction. The modern conception of the human has advanced from that of tradition, so the range of concerns is richer. To delve into all that is human is Jia's constant endeavor. From his early character Wang Mantang to a recent one like Han Qixiang, he works on many levels, making us recognize and appreciate the boundless reaches of the human spiritual world. The multifarious human types in China, especially those of society's lower stratum, have always been his key objects of observation and concern as a writer. Over decades he has groped and trudged and tumbled along the rough, roundabout path that has brought him to the present. He has reached the level at which his fiction can purify and cleanse mental state and emotion without contrivance, in an unprecedented way that merges naturalism, mysticism, realism and modernism. In contemporary Chinese literature, he looms as a mountain that no one can skirt without climbing.

We should examine Jia Pingwa the Writer together with Jia Pingwa the Artist. This article merely presents a rough discussion of his short fiction, so it cannot present a vision of

Critique
评论

定难窥全豹。在文化的意义上建构商州和超越商州的贾平

凹，是既有联系又有不同的。从艺术的角度，贾平凹有大量

的中短篇小说被改编成电影、电视剧、戏曲及舞台剧，有着

广泛的社会影响。有着过人天赋而且无比勤奋的贾平凹今后

还会带给我们多少惊喜，现在尚难预料。更遑论贾平凹文学

的研究尚有巨大的空间，说是前途无量大约不是夸大其辞

罢？我们过去印象中，恒星是不动的，只有行星在动。科技

界已经观察到的恒星不仅是发光、发热，恒星也在做不同速

度的运动。我由衷地盼望贾平凹成为一颗光芒四射的恒星。

2013 年

the whole picture. In a cultural sense, the Jia who constructs the fictional world of Shangzhou and the one who transcends it are connected but not equivalent. Due to their artistic merit, a large number of his short stories and novellas have been adapted into movies and TV series, stage plays and dance dramas, thereby broadening their influence on society. Right now it is hard to predict what surprises this outstandingly talented and hard-working writer has in store for us. At any rate, there is still plenty of space in which literary studies on Jia's oeuvre can unfold: to say there are unbounded prospects for research would be no exaggeration. In the past the term "fixed star" gave one the impression of an unmoving celestial body, and only planets were thought of as moving. By now scientists have observed that fixed stars are not just emitters of light and heat: they too move through space at various speeds. It is my heartfelt wish that Jia Pingwa will be recognized as a fixed star sending out beams in all directions.

2013

专访贾平凹

张　杰

张杰：看到您的第 16 部长篇《山本》出版，很多人第

一反应是：贾老师太勤勉了。看到您的小说密密麻麻的字，

尤其是还考虑到您是用纸笔写的，不由更敬佩您的毅力，您

对写作的用情至深。如果让您来形容，写作对您，到底是什

么在吸引着您？是一种表达的快乐，在文字中找到精神家园

An Interview with Jia Pingwa

By Zhang Jie

Translated by Ella Schwalb

Zhang Jie: With the publication of your 16th novel, the lengthy *Shan Ben*, many people's first reaction has been: Master Jia is incredibly industrious. Seeing the densely packed characters of your manuscript—especially given the fact that it is handwritten—one can't help but admire your perseverance, the depth of your devotion to writing. If you had to describe it, what is it that really attracts you to writing? Is it a kind of bliss of expression, the relief of finding a spiritual abode in written

的安心？

贾平凹：写作的过程是与神相会的时候，别人看着辛苦，其实自己身心有一种说不出的愉悦。也是写作了几十年，已经成为习惯，成为生活的一种方式。至于怎么能有那么多东西要写？对待生活要存机警之心，从事写作得生饥饿之感。

张杰：我读您的这部《山本》，最大的感受是，里面有很深厚的生活，氤氲有山林之气。细细密密的行文之中，有人情世故、世道人心。活成一个人所需要的或明显或隐秘的道理。人与自然，人与天地，人与他人，人与时代的关系，牵扯纠缠。在写作过程中，您内心是否也是含混的状态多，还是明镜高悬的状态多些？

贾平凹：写作说到底，都是在写自己。你的能量，你的视野，你对天地自然，对生命的理解决定着作品的深浅和大

language?

Jia Pingwa: The writing process is a moment of communion with the soul. Other people are seeing arduous work, but actually my body and mind have this kind of unspeakable joy. Having written for a few decades, it's already become a habit for me, a way of life. As far as how I can write so much? You must approach life with a perceptive mind and a sensitive heart; to devote yourself to writing you must foster a feeling of hunger.

Zhang Jie: When I read your book *Shan Ben*, the strongest feeling was this very profound life in there, like a dense mountainous forest enshrouded in mist. Within the detailed writing, one finds the ways of people, the ways of the world, the nature of its people and the reasons for human life, whether obvious or hidden. The relationships between man and nature, the world, fellow man, and the times are all interrelated, tangled up in one another. In your writing process, does the state of your heart tend to be more ambiguous, or more clear and discerning?

Jia Pingwa: In the end, it's all about writing yourself. The depth and magnitude of your work is dictated by your energy, your field of vision, your understanding of nature and

小。我是写了几十年的人了，又到了这般年纪，有些东西我只能看透，有我的体悟，但更多的东西我也在迷惑，企图去接近它，了解它，向往它。

张杰：贾老师的小说，篇幅都是很长，但我从中都能看到散文的影子，看到诗歌的影子。包括我在内的很多读者也是贾老师散文的热情爱好者。您的散文自成一格，简淡古拙之美。您是如何看待散文、小说、诗歌这古学体裁的区别与联系的？在您个人的写作中，您是如何融合这三者的？

贾平凹：我在写作中不愿意把体裁分得那么明明了了，任何作品的境界都是一样的，仅仅在长短上，结构不同而已。不是说要故意如何融合，只是随心所欲，信手而写。

张杰：贾老师的行文之中，能读出古典文学的底蕴。让我不禁好奇，您一定在读先秦诸子、《诗经》等原典。您练习书法，收藏古物，我想您其实是在养一种气。这种气会流

of life. As someone who has been writing for a few decades, and at this stage of my life, there are some things I will just see right through—I have my experience and insight. However, there are even more things that still leave me puzzled; I am trying to get closer to them, to understand them. I yearn for them.

Zhang Jie: Your novels are very long, but within them all, I can see traces of prose and of poetry. I am among the many readers who are also passionate enthusiasts of your essays, which are unique, having the beauty of a plain, light simplicity. How do you see the distinctions and connections between the genres of essay, fiction, and poetry? In your own personal writing, how do you reconcile the three?

Jia Pingwa: I don't want to make such clear-cut distinctions between genres in my writing. The purview of any piece of writing is the same; they differ in nothing more than length and structure. It's not that I reconcile them on purpose; I'm just following my heart, writing offhand.

Zhang Jie: The fine points of classical literature can be read in your writing style. So I can't help but wonder: you must have studied the original canon of various pre-Qin sages, *The Book of Songs*, etc. You practice calligraphy, you collect antiques—I suppose you're really nurturing a certain air about

传渗透到您的文学中。我可以这么理解吗？民间生活、自然

山川、人物经典或技艺造物，是您的文学世界的源头活水。

可以这么理解吗？

    贾平凹： 可以这么理解。写作、书法、绘画、收藏等

等，这完全出自于爱好，出自于天性，其实审美都是一样

的。我认为从事任何形式的艺术，一定要有现代性、传统

性、民间性，他们是相互作用的。

    张杰： 这几年看您的小说，能感觉到贾老师的小说里逐

渐多了自然与人文的对照思考，多了对山河的亲近和敬畏。

比如您说，"一条龙脉，横亘在那里，提携了长江黄河，统

领着北方南方。这就是秦岭，中国最伟大的山。"您本人有

怎样的自我感受？这种变化，您自己是怎么看待的？

    贾平凹： 初学写作时你觉得你什么都知道，你无所不

能，而愈是写作，愈明白了你的无知和渺小。越写越有了一

you. This air surely transfers, infusing your writing. Could I see it that way? Would you say that the wellspring of your literary world is folklife, natural landscapes, classic characters, and divine craftsmanship?

Jia Pingwa: You could see it that way. Writing, calligraphy, painting, collecting, etc. , these are all born out of interest, out of my natural disposition. In fact that's how all aesthetic taste is. I believe when working on any form of art there must necessarily be an interplay between the modern, the traditional, and the folk.

Zhang Jie: Reading your fiction of the past few years, one gets the sense that you are gradually starting to ponder more and more the contrast between nature and human affairs, that there is more intimacy with and reverence for mountains and rivers. For example your line: "The mountain ridge spans the place eternally like a dragon, guiding the Yangtze and Yellow Rivers, commanding the North and the South. This is the Qinling mountain range, China's grandest mountains." What is your own feeling about this transformation of yours?

Jia Pingwa: When you first learn to write, you think you already know it all, that you're omnipotent. But the more you write, the more you realize your own ignorance and insignificance.

种惊恐，惊恐大自然，惊恐社会，惊恐文字，作品常常是在这种惊恐中完成的，只想把自己的体悟的东西表达出来，而不是仅仅是一个传奇的故事或一些华丽句子去取悦读者。

张杰：这几年，陈忠实先生、红柯先生等陕西籍实力作家的"远行"，让人感慨生命的脆弱、短暂。作为他们的朋友、同行，在某种程度上也是彼此文学的知音，您不可能不被触动。对生死这件事，从哲学上或者现实上来说，贾老师现在是怎样的一个看法？

贾平凹：每个人都将死去，这很正常，但当身边的朋友死去，我们还是会震惊地悲痛。他们的死是死去了我们的一部分。诗人说：生如灿烂之夏花，死如静美之秋叶。活着的时候，要把生命活得圆满。死的时候，要平静和安详，这是人生最理想的。

张杰：一个作家要活在历史中，向历史探寻智慧，同时

The more you write the more you have this kind of awe, the awe of the natural world, the awe of society, the awe of writing. Work is often accomplished in this kind of awe. You may just be trying to express your own experiences and realizations, rather than writing a romance or a few beautiful sentences to please readers.

Zhang Jie: In recent years, many have bemoaned the demise of really powerful Shaanxi writers like Mr. Chen Zhongshi and Mr. Hong Ke, calling to mind the frailty and ephemerality of life. As a friend, colleague, and, on some level, also as one another's literary soul mates, there's no way you've remained unmoved. When it comes to matters of life and death, what kind of view do you take, be it from a philosophical or pragmatic perspective?

Jia Pingwa: Every person will die, it's very ordinary. But when a close friend dies, it still shocks and grieves us; a part of us dies with them. As one poet said: Life is like a splendid summer blossom, death is like a beautiful, motionless autumn leaf. While alive, one must live to the fullest. Facing death, one must be tranquil and serene. This is the most perfect existence.

Zhang Jie: A writer must work within history and seek wisdom from the past, while at the same time live in the

也活在现实中，很难不受当下时代的影响。您"创造"了文学家贾平凹，文学家的贾老师也成就了您。彼此不可分。对您作为一个当下的现实中的人来说，文学有没有帮助您如何更好地与时代相处，起到一定的缓冲作用？

贾平凹：作家是以文学与时代相处的，以作品梳理时代，也在梳理自己，以作品记录时代，也在记录自己。当作品企图影响朝着我们向往的理想前行时，也在提升着作家。当在作品中排遣自己身上毒素时，同时也是在排遣着社会的毒素。

张杰：在《山本》中，您用小说为秦岭作传。巴蜀跟秦岭也关系密切。贾老师近些年来也多次入川来到巴蜀。在您看来，巴蜀，对您的精神吸引力，是怎样的？

贾平凹：巴蜀伟大而且神奇，那里的辉煌历史，那里出现过那么多文学巨人，那里的山水美丽，都是我向往啊。我

current reality, as it's very difficult to remain unaffected by the present era. You "created" the writer Jia Pingwa, and in turn the writer Jia Pingwa has become you—the one cannot be separated from the other. As far as being a person living in our present reality, has literature helped you in any way to better get along with the times, serving as a major buffer?

Jia Pingwa: Authors get along with the times through literature, sorting out their judgment on the era through their work while also sorting out themselves. As they record the times through their work, they are also recording themselves. When writing attempts to influence the pilgrimage towards our ideals, this brings with it the writer's own pilgrimage. When you expel the poison from your own soul in a piece of writing, you are simultaneously driving off the poisons of our society.

Zhang Jie: In *Shan Ben*, you're writing a biography of the Qinling Mountain in the form of fiction, and Bashu is also intimately tied to these mountains. These past few years, you have frequently gone to Sichuan, to Bashu. What kind of magnetic pull do you see Bashu as having on your spirit?

Jia Pingwa: Bashu is both grand and mystical. There is a glorious history, there are many literary giants who have come out of Bashu, and there is the beauty of its landscapes. I yearn

已十多次游历过许多地方，今后仍要多去。游名川、谈奇书、见大人，以养我的浩然之气啊！

张杰：您的女儿贾浅浅也写诗，而且出了诗集，受到诗歌圈的专业人士的好评。对于女儿的文学才华，作为父亲，您在旁边观察，内心是怎样的感受？

贾平凹：对于女儿显露出的才华，我既欣慰，但又担心，因为进入文坛，压力很大，是是非非也多。我希望她幸福、自在、平安就好。

2018 年

for it all. I've gone on more than 10 trips traveling to many different places there, and I still want to go back for more. Traveling along famous rivers, discussing wonderful books, meeting the greats: these are all good nourishments for cultivating my noble spirit!

Zhang Jie: Your daughter Jia Qianqian also writes poetry and has been well-received by the professional poetry circle. How do you feel as a father, observing your daughter's literary talent from the sidelines?

Jia Pingwa: As far as my daughter's talent being on display, I am both gratified and anxious because there's a lot of pressure as well as a lot of squabbling when you get into literary circles. I wish just for her happiness, comfort, and peace.

2018